FROM CHICKEN COOP
TO MOUNTAINTOP:

ALL GOOD!

FROM CHICKEN COOP TO MOUNTAINTOP:

ALL GOOD!

by

Felix Holmes Jr.

For more information:
Stephen F. Austin State University Press
P.O. Box 13007 SFA Station
Nacogdoches, Texas 75962
sfapress@sfasu.edu
www.sfasu.edu/sfapress

Book design: Shaina Hawkins
Cover design: Shaina Hawkins
Distributed by Texas A&M Consortium
www.tamupress.com

LIBRARY OF CONGRESS CATALOGING-IN-PUBLICATION DATA
Holmes, Felix Jr.
From Chicken Coop to Mountaintop: All Good!/Felix Holmes Jr.

ISBN: 978-1-62288-301-1

Cover Photo: Remembering what my first job was like: Thanks to Ricky Lout of Lout's Chicken Farm, who let me visit his chicken house and reminisce about the past.

TABLE OF CONTENTS

This book is dedicated to:

Gloria Fay Holmes

my loving, compassionate, optimistic soul mate of 40 years
who always gives me that extra support when it is most needed.

A NOTE FROM THE AUTHOR

When I decided to write my autobiography, I embarked on a journey that allowed me, with the assistance of documents, photographs, and lots of conversations with people who knew me as a child and young man, to revisit my past. At first I thought it would be very difficult to write about my childhood, but I discovered that it is possible to jog your memory so that you are able to recall events and people from the past. My wife, Gloria Fay Holmes, assisted me greatly as she asked for the details of events I would initially bring up in conversations we were having regarding my autobiography. With her questions, I was excited to find that I could actually recapture and "picture" what happened years ago.

In telling my life story, I hope to help others understand that if you work hard, success can be attained. I firmly believe that it is your work ethic, more than your gender, race, or level of education, which determines your success in life. Having a good attitude, coming to the job prepared to work, putting forth your best effort, and being punctual are the components of my "Work Creed." This is what I have brought to any job I have ever had and what helped me to advance during my career with the U.S. Forest Service.

As you read my autobiography, I think you will be able to identify the values that dictate the way I act and how I came to acquire them. I value and believe in being honest, working hard, never giving up, showing others respect, being a good neighbor, and having integrity. I have often told others that "a good name means more than a dollar in your pocket."

My wife had always said that, after retirement, she wanted to help me write this book because she felt I had a story to relate about perseverance in the face of obstacles in my lifetime. We undertook this writing project as a legacy to our children and grandchildren, hoping it will help them to understand why we have always believed outstanding character and good work ethics put you on the road to success.

The title chosen for this book was suggested by my wife. As she explained, I went from being a "chicken-catcher" in my youth to climbing mountainsides to fight wildfires as an adult during my 36 years with the U.S. Forest Service. I agreed with her that *From Chicken Coop to Mountaintop* seemed a fitting title for my life story.

—Felix "Bubba" Holmes Jr.

Proving I still have what it takes to put chickens in a coop.
(Photo taken 2016 at Lout's Chicken Farm)

FORWARD

I just wanted to say what an honor it was to format this book. Felix asked me for advice on how to write his autobiography, and quite frankly, I hadn't done anything like this before. So I looked on the internet and also looked at some autobiographies, and met with Felix and Gloria. During the meeting, I felt that both understood quite clearly the reasons for doing an autobiography and were looking for some reassurance that they were on the right track. When I received the manuscript, I was impressed with the clarity of the book. There were only very minor editorial corrections I had to make with the text and images. Felix had done it! He had done it with the help of Gloria and Nancy Stone, and of course, all the people who contributed their testimonies about their relationship with Felix. Finally, I'd like to thank Jerry Williams of Stephen F. Austin State University's Center for Regional Heritage Research for printing this book as part of the Center's publication activities.

—George E. Avery
Stephen F. Austin State University

SECTION ONE:
MY CHILDHOOD AND TEEN YEARS

I turned 60 years old in 2014 and at the urging of my wife, family, and friends, I have finally decided to write my autobiography. It is a legacy which I wish to pass on to future generations of my family – the opportunity to know what my childhood was like, where some of our "family" stories came from, and the people and events that influenced the man I became. The dates I cite are all accurate, since I have documentation for them in the form of birth/death certificates, marriage records, cemetery records, and court documents, but where I may have made occasional errors is the chronological order for some events in this autobiography and the exact age I was at the time. What happened is true, but I lack the specific dates, especially with regard to memories from my childhood. I have used school annuals, historical dates (i.e., beginning of school integration in Hemphill), and other resources to assist me in being as chronologically accurate as possible.

My parents, Felix Holmes and Louella Dupree, were married on November 26, 1940, in Sabine County, Texas. Fourteen years later, on May 5, 1954, I was born at Memorial Hospital in Nacogdoches, Texas. Although I was the third child (and only son) born to my mother, I have no childhood memories of my oldest sister because she was already grown and had moved out before I was born. The only thing my mama ever told me about my birth was that the doctor who delivered me injured my jaw. We spent five days in the hospital before Mama was able to bring me home to our twenty-acre farm in the Thomas Johnson community near Hemphill, Texas.

Louella Dupree Holmes

My daddy, Felix Holmes Sr., was 60 years old when I was born (he died when I was six years old). People who knew him well have told me he was a hard worker who laughed a lot and told jokes. Then they usually go on to say except for work habits and the way I dress, I'm definitely my father's son. They credit me with working much harder during my life than he ever did. The reference to appearance refers to the fact that when my daddy left the house, he was always dressed in a white shirt and khaki pants. A "sport" was the way he was described to me. Maybe that's what caught my mama's eye.

She was 28 years younger than him when they got married. He was born on October 13, 1893, in Milam, Texas, and she was born on July 17, 1921.

Our farm was directly across the road from Thomas Johnson School, the black school in Hemphill, Texas. On our property, my daddy built a café with a barbecue pit next to it, where he cooked the pork, beef, and chicken sold at the café. Teachers and kids from the school ate there, as well as customers from the Thomas Johnson community and nearby Hemphill. Lots of people came for the barbecue and my mom's tasty chili dogs; she later passed on some of her cooking secrets to me. As an adult, I became known for the ability to make what some folks described as, "the best barbecue I've ever eaten." My mama ran the café during the day, while my daddy worked at one of his other jobs: chauffeuring business owners in Hemphill, driving a school bus, or working as a mechanic at the Hemphill Ford Motor Company. It makes me proud that, to this day, a toolbox with his name carved on it still sits in the garage behind the original showroom of the building that housed the Hemphill Ford Motor Company. In addition to his jobs in the community, Daddy raised chickens, hogs, and vegetables on his twenty-acre truck farm.

My daddy died of lung cancer on November 30, 1960, just months after I started school. Though I have difficulty remembering what he was like, I've been told I was usually sitting up in the front seat right next to him when he went driving in his blue Buick (the car he owned prior to his death). I do recall climbing up in his bed and lying next to him during the time he was sick, and I can still picture in my mind all the school buses lined up at the Macedonia Church, while the students from Thomas Johnson School attended his funeral. At the time of my dad's death, my parents had been married 20 years.

My daddy's death brought some big changes in my life. With no father in my home to guide me, I could have easily gotten into lots of trouble, especially since I was like most kids – willing to try anything at least one time. Luckily, there were men in the community willing to step in and assume responsibility for teaching me the skills and values that would allow me to grow into a productive, responsible adult. I also credit these men with teaching me courtesy and neighborliness. They never hesitated to step in and become the "father" figure when a "whupping" was necessary, and believe me, I got plenty of them. I wish to note here that "whupping" or "whipping" were words used when I was growing up; today, that action would be called a "spanking." It was never a "beating," just a plain old-fashioned spanking.

Five men, in particular, helped develop my work ethic. Joe Dupree, Coolridge Coleman, Clarence Winn, Willie "Sweetie" Bell, and Phillip Gandy gave me opportunities to acquire and use a variety of work-related skills. I learned a number of "life" lessons from these men, several of which I will share in this autobiography. Although there were times when I played with other kids, I spent a lot of my childhood finding ways to earn money so I could take care of myself. Very early in my youth, I made a conscious decision that I would always support myself, regardless of the nature of the job it took to accomplish that.

With my daddy's passing, I had to assume responsibility for some of the chores he had performed at home. It became my job to go up to the Commodities House at Beanville (about one mile from the courthouse in Hemphill) once a month with my mom to get groceries. That was a place where poor families could go to get food items like beans, rice, and cheese to supplement their diet. My mom had sold Daddy's car because she couldn't afford to keep it, so we walked nearly five miles (round trip) to bring home the food. At the time, I was six years old. I also became responsible for hauling water from the neighbor's well anytime it rained and made our well water dirty. When we needed a fire, I took an axe and went out into the woods to cut "rich lighter pine," hauling this kindling home in a "croker" sack (a bag made from burlap or a similar fabric). To keep the fire going, I'd cut oak wood with a crosscut saw and cart it to the house. That croker sack got a lot of use. When I was a little older, my mama started sending me to the Commodities House on my own. A neighborhood friend often went with me. We'd leave the house before dawn, arriving in time to help Miss Lois Smith open up for the day. At the end of the day, she'd give us some extra food for helping her. We'd fill our croker sacks and start for home, dragging the sacks along behind us. We took lots of play breaks along the way but made it home before dark.

Since it was too difficult for my mom to run the café without my dad's assistance, she had rented it out to Herman Emanuel who also, each day, hauled a truckload of men down to Pineland, Texas, to work at the Temple Sawmill. On Friday nights, Herman had me clean the vehicle he used, a green Chevrolet pickup with a camper on the back. He gave me some pocket change for doing this job each week. In 1964, Herman was shot and killed at the café. My mama and I were sitting on our front porch when we saw a man drive up to the café and shoot Herman through a window. Rather than try to rent the café again, Mama sold it and two acres of land to my cousin, Joe Dupree, for fifty dollars. Since the acreage she sold him was located about ¼ mile from the site of the café, Dupree had to have the building moved. He turned our old café into his home, and it remains there today adjacent to my property.

August of the same year my daddy died, I had started first grade at the Thomas Johnson School. I was in Mrs. Celia P. Greer's class (at that time, there was no kindergarten). In second grade, I had Mrs. Leachie Canton. She was known to holler at you and pull your ear if she couldn't get your attention. Naturally, my favorite school activity was recess. I can remember playing cowboys out in the woods behind the school where there were two creek beds that crossed an old railroad bed. We'd cut branches to use for guns and pretend to shoot at each other from the creek beds. Shooting marbles and playing hopscotch were other games we played at recess. Mrs. Ruthie Malone was my third grade teacher; a former veteran, she disciplined us with a razor strap. Knowing I was going to get the strap a day before it happened, I would stuff my back pockets with paper before going to school. Unfortunately for me, she would always find the paper, remove it, and then whip me, probably harder due to my "pocket-stuffing" trick. When Mr. Gaskin, the owner of a shoe shop in town, started putting taps on shoes and boots, we headed to town to have them placed on our shoes. It was so much fun to tap on the cement walk leading up to the school door. Unfortunately we had to leave the shoes outside which meant most of us were barefooted in the classroom. With integration, the problem was handled differently by the Hemphill Schools; we were sent to Mr. Gaskin's shop to have the taps removed before we could enter any building, since going shoeless in the classroom was not an option there.

Here I am in front of Thomas Johnson School. Notice the cement walk —
it extends out and widens, making it perfect for toe-tapping fun.

One of the men influential in my life was a teacher at Thomas Johnson
School. Known as "Prof," Coolridge Coleman was the agriculture teacher
and football/basketball coach. He taught in a separate building adjacent to the
main school building. David Lee Thomas, a friend my age I played with after
school, was his brother-in-law. We would hang around the AG shop waiting
for "Prof" to finish his paperwork. Then we would follow him around in
the community, whether he was going up to the store or to his truck farm
on Clarence Winn's property (just down the road from the school). He had
acreage where he grew sugar cane, corn, and other vegetables.

Mr. Coolridge Coleman in his corn field

A "life" lesson I learned from Mr. Coleman had to do with my decision to go into business for myself. One evening when David and I knew Mr. Coleman was not around, we went into his cane field, and each of us cut an armful of cane. Sneaking through the woods, we came out in back of the school gym where we left the cane. The next day at lunchtime, we started selling sugar cane to the other kids. The next thing I knew Mr. Coleman was standing in front of me demanding to know where we had gotten the cane. The business closed abruptly when Mr. Coleman took us in the AG shop and whipped us with a razor strap. He informed us he never wanted to catch us stealing again. His advice: always ask for something you want, and never take anything without permission. Later on, our business reopened when Mr. Coleman allowed us to use the back of his pickup to haul cane from his field up to the school, so we could sell it. That lesson stuck with me – I never stole another thing in my life. Oops, wait a minute...I take that back! I stole the girl I married from her potential suitors in San Augustine County (Hemphill High School and San Augustine High School, located in adjacent counties, have always had a long-standing rivalry when it comes to sports and girls).

Prior to integration, Thomas Johnson School had its own football and basketball teams. Coolridge Coleman was the coach for the T.J. Hawks, and he decided David Lee and I were going to be his basketball and football managers. I believe I was either in third or fourth grade at the time. Whenever there were basketball games, as his managers, we had to use push brooms to clean the floor at halftime and at the conclusion of the game. In exchange for our sweeping, we got into the games for free. During football season, we had to fill up soda water bottles with water from the school well, put them in crates, and carry them to the field for the players to have during the games. It's amazing what a job title and the offer of free admission can get a kid to do.

Since I had spent a lot of time hanging out at my parents' café as a small youngster, I was familiar with the male adults in the community that knew my daddy. I liked being around them and watching what they were doing – that seemed to be the easiest way for me to learn something new. Many of them, including Clarence Winn, played cards and dominos at Mattie's Café, located across the road from our café. You could catch a game there most nights and on weekends, they often played all through the night. I started going over there around the time I was in fifth or sixth grade, and they let me play with them. When I wasn't earning money one place or another or lending a helping hand to an elderly person in the community, I was playing dominos with the guys at Mattie's, and, yes, I did occasionally stay up all night to play with them.

On Saturday nights, Mattie's Cafe often had a live band. Lots of people from the community came to the café to eat, drink, and enjoy the music played by these bands. I remember one band, known as the Johnny Cadillac Band, coming in from Louisiana. Their music made you jump up and dance, which is exactly what I did. Before I knew it, I had a circle of people around me encouraging me to keep on dancing. My feet were flying out beneath me; I was even doing the splits and popping up with little effort. My performance went to a new level when the older people started throwing coins on the floor to keep me dancing. Of course, with the money came other pint-size dancers who wanted in on the action. When the song was over, we all raced to gather up the coins. I loved those moments of "fame."

During this same time period, I was briefly involved in an activity that was very exciting for a young boy. I was the "runner" for a bootlegger! Since I was out and about so much in the community, no one really paid any attention to me, but I sure heard and saw a lot of things a kid might not be expected to know. Our community bootlegger periodically made a liquor run to Louisiana and when he came back, he would hide the bottles on our property – he figured the law wouldn't think to look on the Widow Holmes' land. Because I was "on" to his hiding place, he started using me to run and get a bottle anytime he had a customer. He paid me for each bottle I fetched. I don't remember exactly what I got paid when I brought him a bottle or how long my "life of crime" lasted, but it sure was fun at the time.

When Willie "Sweetie" Bell became our next-door neighbor (he moved here from San Augustine, Texas), I had the opportunity to learn some blacksmith skills. In addition to being a blacksmith and wood craftsman, Mr. Sweetie worked for the Sturgis Sawmill. He would bring home the grab hooks from the mill that needed repairing, and I would help operate the forge, keeping the fire at a constant temperature by turning the handle on it. Mr. Sweetie had stressed to me the importance of keeping the temperature constant while working on a project. However, I remember one occasion when he decided he needed a break and went in the house. Thinking I had a break coming too, I stopped turning the handle and started playing around. I bet you can guess what happened when Mr. Sweetie came out of his house and discovered the temperature of his fire had dropped. Yup! A whipping!

Mr. Sweetie carved gunstocks, ax and other tool handles, as well as walking sticks. He'd send me out to find hickory wood to use to make these items. I knew slick bark hickory grew best along a sandy ridge, so that's where I would look. He showed me how to use an ax to split the hickory into workable pieces; then he taught me to use a small hatchet to remove the bark from the wood. To shave the wood smooth, Mr. Sweetie would use a piece of old window glass. Eventually he taught me to heat metal and bend it into hooks and similar objects, but he never taught me woodcarving. He'd say, "Boy, your head ain't made right to learn how to make the tool handles." He did teach me how to make horse whips by plaiting strips of leather together that he ordered from a leather supplier. I guess he figured my head "was right enough" to complete a whip but not a carved handle.

Mr. Sweetie had a field about 1½ miles down the road from his house where he planted peas, watermelon, and corn. He kept a mule at his house that he used to work his field. On days when he intended to use the mule after he returned from the sawmill, he'd tell me to walk it down to the field before school and tie it there for him. "Don't run the mule" were the words I heard every time he told me to do this because a tired mule will balk. Once he headed for work, I'd run that mule as fast as I could make him go, so I could get back up to the schoolyard and have some playtime. One day the sawmill sent its workers home early in the day, and Mr. Sweetie found his mule, tied up and soaking wet from his run down the road. Unfortunately, there hadn't been enough time for the mule to cool down. I suspect Mr. Sweetie knew I had been running the mule all along, but he hadn't had any evidence with which to confront me. When I showed up at the field after school, imagine my surprise when the first words out of his mouth were "Did you run that mule today, boy? Don't lie to me!" My honest response to his question got me another whipping! I never ran that mule again – couldn't take a chance on Mr. Sweetie getting home early.

Mr. Sweetie Bell was the first one to give me some advice about money, and it always stuck with me. Since he was also a barber in addition to his other occupations, I figured he had enough businesses going to be taken seriously when it came to money matters. One day he said, "Boy, come here. I know you ain't got any sense, but here's what you do with the money you earn. When you get paid, pay yourself first." He went on to explain that what he meant was you save a bit of everything you earn: "If you get a dollar, you save 10 cents; if you get $100, you save $10.00." I started following Mr. Sweetie's advice and later understood the value of his words.

Mr. Sweetie cut hair Thursday and Friday evening and all day Saturday. When he first moved to our community, he cut hair on his porch as long as the weather was tolerable; in bad weather he moved to his living room. He had two cowhide chairs about table size that he used for barbering. For a child, he would stack one chair on top of the other. Later he built a house and garage next to his field with a barber shop attached to the garage. The shop was furnished with a wooden bench along the wall and an actual barbershop chair.

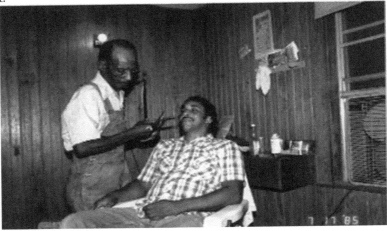

Willie "Sweetie" Bell cutting my hair

When Willie "Sweetie" Bell died in 1993, his son, Joe Bell, gave me all of his blacksmith tools because he knew I was the one who had worked with him in his blacksmith shop. I also have the barber chair and wooden bench from his shop. I loaned his tools to the Stone Fort Museum in Nacogdoches for a blacksmith shop they set up in June 2011 as part of a display entitled: Cornerstones of the Community: African American History in Eastern Texas. In February 2013, during Black History Month, the tools were part of an exhibit: Celebrating African American Heritage and Culture with Love. I later made the decision to donate the tools to the Stone Fort Museum's permanent collection, so others could enjoy this bit of history.

Phillip Gandy, the owner of Gandy's Cleaners in Hemphill, started building chicken houses on the land he owned adjacent to my mom's property around the time I was in fourth or fifth grade. He came looking for kids to water and feed the bitties (baby chicks), and since I needed money to help take care of my mom and sister, I went to work there in the evenings. I worked every other evening; it was often nine or ten o'clock at night before I got home. After the chicks were older, instead of feeding them, I cleaned the troughs and removed the dead chickens from the three houses he had built there. Mr. Gandy was paying me 75 cents per hour; on Saturdays, I went up to his cleaners and washed and cleaned clothes. His son, Mark Gandy, worked right alongside me. On Sundays, I fed cattle at the Gandy farm.

On the days when I wasn't working for Mr. Gandy, I worked for Clarence Winn who had both a lawn mowing and firewood business. In the summer, we cut lawns; one of his customers was the Macedonia Church, and it took all day to do their mowing. It sure got hot pushing that lawn mower around the grounds. In the fall, we cut firewood. I was paid one dollar for throwing a rick of wood on the truck, another dollar for throwing it off the truck, and two dollars if the customer wanted it stacked. When I would get the money I'd earned, I would buy food and bring it home. I also used some of the money to buy school clothes when I needed them. I was willing to do anything to support myself because I never wanted to depend on anyone else. Once I was older, I never felt the world owed me a living – just the chance to make a living.

With the integration of schools in 1964, the high school students at Thomas Johnson moved to Hemphill High School, and I acquired a "day" job during the school year. For the previous two years, I had been responsible for turning on the switch for the water pump at school. Every morning I would climb up on a block to throw the breaker. If I didn't have another job to do, I would also help Butler Roberts, our janitor, clean classrooms. He sometimes gave me a dollar for helping him. However, when the older students moved to Hemphill High School, our cafeteria no longer prepared the food for lunch at Thomas Johnson. Instead, the food was sent over daily in large pots from the Hemphill School. Several of us students were hired to dump the trays and empty the pots into garbage cans at the end of the lunch period. We were allowed to take home leftovers (this often became my supper); Clarence Winn hauled off what was in the garbage cans for his hogs. I received a weekly check in the amount of four dollars from Hemphill High School for my "day" job.

I never missed the opportunity to learn something that would help me make it through life. Joe Dupree, my cousin, was the man who taught me my mechanic skills. I was probably between the ages of 10-12 when we started working on cars together. After he was through with his day job at the Hemphill Ford Motor Company, we would work on cars in the evening at his house. By this time, my mom owned another car – Joe's daddy had given her a 1953 Chevrolet. I would take it out on the road (no license, of course) and end up stripping the clutch while attempting to race it. This is where I learned another "life" lesson. Joe would make me take out the transmission and replace the clutch on my own, without any assistance from him. I guess I was a slow learner because I stripped that clutch at least three times before the "life" lesson sunk in: take care of what you own, and you'll save yourself both time and money. I guess that's why, to this day, I take care of the things I own, especially my vehicles. Though I had learned to build a bicycle from parts I salvaged from the dump, Joe was the one who bought me my first brand new bicycle. However, when I tore up a tire purposely skidding out on the road, he made me earn the money to buy another tire. Meantime, I had no wheels, so I was forced to walk everywhere. Another lesson learned!

My mom had decided to buy a pig from Joe Dupree to fatten up for slaughter. We were keeping him in the smokehouse behind our house. One day he got loose, and a dog tore him up. I moved him up on the back porch and started tending to his wounds. For 50 cents, I was able to buy a "purple spray" that I knew people used on animal cuts and sores. His wounds were healing, but I was still worried about him. I started leaving the door to my bedroom, which opened onto the porch, cracked a bit so he could get inside. He definitely became a pet when I started calling him "Joe." When Joe was big enough to butcher, there was no way that was going to happen. Eventually, my mom sold him to someone else with the understanding that "Joe" was my first and last pet (though my mom had several pet dogs at different times during my childhood).

My mom's parents lived in San Augustine County in the Black Ankle community, about 20 miles north of where we lived near Hemphill. My grandparents, Angelo Dupree and Elizabeth Coutee Dupree, had moved to

Texas from Natchitoches, Louisiana. Several times a month, my mom, sister, and I would travel with Aunt Jerri Lee, Uncle Carter, and their six children to see Grandpa and Grandma. On Friday evening, eleven of us would pile into my uncle's old Chevrolet station wagon and drive up to Black Ankle. We'd stay with my grandparents until Sunday afternoon. The back floorboard on my uncle's car was rusted out and once we were on our way, it was great fun to drop paper scraps and other items out of the hole and then look back to see where they ended up.

During the weekend, my grandpa kept us busy picking cotton, feeding the cows and chickens, hauling wood for the stove, and fetching water from his well. I can remember holding the bucket for him while he milked his cows. Those cows produced some bad tasting milk, especially when they got into bitterweed. However, we had no choice but to drink it. The rule was you ate and drank what was put on the table at mealtime, or you went hungry. There were three meals served each day – once you ate a meal, you were not allowed in the kitchen until the next mealtime. If you needed a drink of water, you could go as far as the water shelf near the door to the kitchen. That's where you'd find the water bucket and dipper, sitting on the top shelf, with the basin for washing up directly under it on another shelf.

I had two uncles and aunts that lived near my grandparents. Uncle Jefferson B. Jenkins (we called him Uncle B) and Aunt Annie B. Jenkins had five sons. Uncle Ennis and Aunt Lulean Jenkins had 16 children. Jefferson and Ennis were brothers, and their wives were sisters. Uncle B's family relied on a spring for their drinking water. We made lots of trips to and from that spring, especially in the summer. Uncle B taught us how to make a wooden wagon. He would cut "wheels" from a red oak tree, and we would use 2x4's as axles. We'd nail a wooden wheel on the end of each axle; then use another 2x4 to create a base for the wooden seat. An old fan belt nailed to the front of the wagon allowed us to pull each other around in the yard. Other than eating and sleeping in the house, we spent all our time outdoors. This was where I rode a goat for the first time. Old Billie was a family pet and if more than one of us tried to ride him at the same time, he'd just sit down, as one by one, we slid off his back. With one child on his back, he'd treat you to a bouncy ride all over the place.

If you added up all the cousins when we were at Black Ankle, there could be as many as 29 of us together on a weekend. On Saturdays, we'd walk down to Arvie Neal's Grocery to buy soda water and penny candy. Either my grandpa or one of the uncles would give us some money to spend there. I can remember the huge Baby Ruth bars you could get for five cents or the corn suckers that might have money in them. These suckers were shaped like a shucked ear of corn and came in different flavors. We called them "coin" suckers because if you were lucky, you might find a nickel, dime, or quarter in one and be able to go back and buy another sucker.

After dark, we'd roam up and down the country roads. The older cousins loved disappearing into the brush ahead of us – with no street lights, it was truly pitch black at night. Once we had walked past their hiding spot, they'd come crashing out on the road and carry on like they were "haints". Their antics had us running down the road, screaming at the top of our lungs. It was especially effective when we took the road that ran past the cemetery. Night was the perfect time for the older cousins to swipe sweet, juicy watermelons from a neighbor's field. They would drop them on the road to break them up in pieces. We would fill our bellies and wipe away the evidence before heading back to our grandparents' house.

This photo of Arvie Neal's Grocery was taken in 2014.
Though the store has been closed for a number of years, the building is still standing.

This is the house I had moved into on the Gandy Farm when I was eleven years old. Though this is a recent photo (2014), the house looks about the same as when I lived there almost 49 years ago.

When I was eleven years old, I moved into a small house on the Gandy Farm. Mr. Gandy needed someone living on the premises to check on the chickens and assist with cleaning the chicken houses between batches of bitties. Usually you had two weeks to get everything ready before a new shipment of chicks arrived. The house I lived in had one bedroom and a small kitchen/living area. Casey Hickman, a friend who was a year older, stayed with me part of the time. I would stop by to check on my mom and make sure she had wood and water, but I was no longer sleeping at home. For meals, I often cooked beans and wieners. I had discovered I could buy ten cans of beans for $1.00. Occasionally, I would catch and skin a chicken and boil it up for several meals. When I was fourteen years old, Phillip Gandy helped me get a hardship driver's license. Then he allowed me to use a yellow GMC pickup he owned. I lived at the farm for 3-4 years. When I started working for the county the summer before my sophomore year in high school, I moved back in with my mama.

Thinking about my hardship driver's license reminds me of the cat-

and- mouse game I played for several years with a highway patrolman named George Clark. As I mentioned earlier, I had been driving my mama's 1953 Chevrolet up and down the roads in our community since the age of ten or eleven. George Clark had taken to sitting at the intersection of Hwy. 83 and Thomas Johnson Road in an attempt to catch me coming down the road. Once you turned onto Hwy. 83, you were out of our community. Anytime I rounded the curve near my house and spotted his vehicle parked down the road, I'd immediately pull up into the neighbor's yard and hide the car behind her house. Being elderly and hard-of-hearing, she had no idea I was doing that. Then I'd walk home and wait for Officer Clark to leave. One day he and I both got to the intersection at the same time. I pulled out in front of him, raced down Hwy. 83 for several miles, and then cut through the woods on a dirt road that really kicked up the dust but led me back home. He never showed up at my house so I guess I left him "in the dust." Shortly after that incident, I got my license and who should I run into going through town but George Clark. Pulling me over, he said, "I've got your a** now. You've been running from me all this time." Imagine the kick I got out of being able to hand him my legal license to drive.

Porter Halbert was the poultry processing plant in Bronson that picked up the chickens from Mr. Gandy's farm. They were always looking for males to catch chickens for them. The job involved working through the night to remove the chickens from the houses and load them on a truck. The work was done at night because it was cooler and the chickens would be roosting; it was important to keep them calm to avoid having them panic and smother each other. I signed up to be a "chicken catcher." Each house held 12,000 chickens and I'd get paid $2.00 for each 1,000 chickens I caught. Usually 10-12 individuals were assigned to a house. We'd start at dusk and finish somewhere between 2-5:00 a.m. Once the truck arrived, the chicken coops were unloaded, and we started to work. I'd catch four chickens per hand and put them in a coop. Each coop held 24 chickens. Adults loaded the coops on the truck. Halbert's picked up chickens from farms as far away as Center, Texas, to the north and Newton, Texas, to the south. Once hired by them, you were welcome to work six nights a week if you desired. A truck would stop in our community and pick up workers on their way to a chicken farm. I can remember it wasn't unusual to get back home just in time to take a bath before heading to school.

As you may have realized, based on what I've told you, I wasn't one to sit still for any period of time. I was on the go, doing as many things as possible in a single day. This is the way I functioned well into my early 50's when my body finally started telling me to slow down. As a child and then a teen, I often got by with very little sleep. If my mind was on something I wanted to accomplish, there was no sense in going to bed because I would just lie there tossing and turning; I still have that problem today. I'm sure that lack of sleep caused me to miss out on lots of learning in the classroom. My wife is a teacher, and she has observed firsthand children who fight to stay awake in class and as a result, really struggle in school. Obviously if I was up most of the night catching chickens, I wasn't getting enough sleep for a kid. Many of the whuppings I got in school were for sleeping in class, until my teachers realized what I was doing at night. They didn't let up on me, but I was assigned a study hall after lunch where I was given the last twenty minutes to put my head down – I always went right to sleep.

My mom was hit by a car on August 2, 1968, when I was fourteen years old. I was standing in front of Harvey White's Café, across the road from our house, watching as she walked home along the shoulder of the road. She had been visiting a neighbor. She had her dog "Woofie" with her. I saw the car come up behind her and heard the thud as she was knocked to the ground. As I ran down the road to her, the car pulled into the parking area by the café; the driver didn't even bother to walk down and check on her. Mama had a broken left hip and other injuries. An ambulance took her to Memorial Hospital in Lufkin. I rode in the ambulance with her and stayed in the hospital, sleeping on the floor under her bed, until she was released. She was hospitalized for six weeks and when she came home, she was in a wheelchair.

My sister, Gloria Lamerle, and I were the ones who took care of Mama. Gloria was three years older than me (she was born in 1951). I was still living at the Gandy farm, but I would get up and go to my mama's to make her breakfast before going to school. After school, I would haul wood and water when necessary. One day after cooking my mom's breakfast, I forgot to turn off the burner when I went in to feed her. When I came back to the kitchen, the skillet was on fire. As I grabbed it and ran to the back door, I spilled some of the hot grease on my feet. The burns were so bad I missed the rest of the school year. I used black oil and sulfa to treat the burns because I couldn't afford to go to a doctor. To this day, you can still see the scars on my feet. My mom was in a wheel chair and then a walker for almost a year before she was able to walk again.

Once I got to high school, I had a variety of work experiences. The summer between my freshman and sophomore year, I worked for Commissioner Rob Smith on a road crew. I was paid $1.35 per hour to clean out culverts. On one occasion, I can remember being stranded out in the woods until after quitting time because the driver of the truck I was assigned to decided to go skinny-dipping in Toledo Bend Lake. I was sure glad Commissioner Smith came looking for us.

For two summers, I was part of the Youth Conservation Corp. I was assigned to work for the U.S. Forest Service. In fact, during my second summer of work, I started seriously thinking about getting on permanently with the Forest Service after graduation. I really liked working outside. We cleaned bathrooms at the parks, did mowing, picked up litter, dug holes to set fence posts, and painted signs. Getting to pull lily pads out of a swimming area on a hot summer day sure didn't seem like work. The summer we dug fence post holes, I was assigned to work with James Mattox, a Timber Stand Improvement (TSI) foreman for the Forest Service. Our crew was responsible for digging holes for gates at Indian Mounds Recreation Area. At the end of our work day, we would put water in plastic containers to freeze for use in our drinking water the next day. Before heading out to the park, we would "pop" the chunks of ice out of their plastic containers and use them in our water cooler. One day, some of the kids on the crew stuck soda cans in the ice water. When Mr. Mattox realized what they had done, he told them they were not to do that again – he felt it contaminated the drinking water. The next day, those same kids ignored what he had said and again put their soda cans in the drinking water. Normally in addition to our lunch break, we got several drink breaks a day. On this particular day, however, Mr. Mattox did not give us a break in the morning and when lunchtime came, he stood in front of us and dumped both our ice water and the sodas on the ground. When he ordered us back to work at the end of the lunch break, he told us we had lost our iced drinks for the day because we had not followed directions. A short time later, he called me over and gave me a cold drink from his water jug, saying he knew I had listened to him and was not involved. When several days passed with no sodas in the drinking water, Mr. Mattox managed to find an old cooler to be used for sodas. I suspect the "soda can" boys would have had that cooler right away if they had listened to Mr. Mattox. As a teen, I usually chose to listen and follow directions, though I was as tempted as the next guy to do what I saw others doing. However, I had realized that, inevitability, someone observes your behavior, whether you realize it or not, and appropriate consequences result. You're either rewarded or punished for your actions.

When Coolridge Coleman got a tree planting contract through the U.S. Forest Service, I was one of his high school students who hand-planted trees during Christmas vacation. On weekends during the school year, I'd pick up jobs hauling hay for different farmers. I was paid ten cents per bale, provided

I loaded it on the wagon, took it to the barn, and unloaded it. Hemphill Café, across from the courthouse in Hemphill, had a spot behind it where guys could gather if they were looking for work. People would come by and pick you up to do odd jobs for them. I was able to get some lawn work and other handyman jobs by standing there. I even remember working on a well-digging crew for Red Cotton. After school, I would often check in at the Fuller Feed and Dried Goods Store, just off the square in Hemphill, to see if a truck had come in from Shreveport, Louisiana. These trucks brought in 50 and 100 pound sacks of feed that needed to be unloaded and stacked in the store. By the way, the building that housed the store still exists – it's next to the Hemphill Volunteer Fire Department and is presently being used as a restaurant. I'd also unload sacks and boxes of food at the Commodities House. Jessie Moody, a city employee responsible for picking up the food in Lufkin, would pay us to unload the truck. The pay was minimal though he would say, "a little bit beat none." My work ethic was such that I was there doing the job for whatever it paid. I don't ever recall turning down any work offered to me.

In eleventh grade, I was in an "on-the-job" training program and assigned to the parts department of the Chevrolet dealer in town (GM Water is located there now). Johnny Poye was the parts manager and when I walked in and introduced myself, he wanted to know if Felix Holmes was my daddy. When I told him "yes," he responded with, "Your daddy sure was a sorry man." After he repeated "sorry man" several times, I hid out in the back, among the shelves, wondering what was in store for me. Hearing him call my name, I reluctantly dragged myself toward the front as he said, "If you're half the man your daddy was, you'll be a good man." It turned out Johnny had known my daddy quite well, and his definition of "sorry" definitely did not match mine. I guess I proved I was a good man because he started waiting until 2:00 p.m., when I would get there from school, to eat his lunch. His wife normally brought him lunch, and he started having her bring me one as well. When we had nothing to do, he'd tell me to lie on a mechanic's dolly and take a nap. I still carry with me the great memories I have of working with men like Johnny Poye who helped "fill in" for the father I lost at an early age.

In My Teens

When it came time to graduate, I was short one credit (probably due to the number of days I missed when I burned my feet). Since I didn't have my diploma, I took off that summer for Lufkin with my Auntie Gloria; I was tired of school and not sure I would go back in the fall. However, when I found out I needed a high school diploma to work for the U.S. Forest Service, I did return to Hemphill the fall of 1972 to get that final credit. I was assigned a typing class at 2:00 p.m. each day for the 1972-73 school year. At the old AG shop at Thomas Johnson School, a Manpower Work Program had been set up to teach a 12-week welding program. The government furnished all the equipment needed, and the teacher came over from Nacogdoches, Texas.

I was enrolled in that program from 7:00 a.m. to shortly before 2:00 p.m., when I would head for my typing class at Hemphill High School. By this time, I was the proud owner of a 1965 four-door Ford. Using money I'd saved, I bought this car from Jamie Payne who operated the Ford dealership in Hemphill. I received my high school diploma on May 31, 1973. Sabine County Judge Royce Smith handed it to me as I marched across the football field during the graduation ceremony.

After graduation, I went to work at the Conoco Station in Hemphill. I mainly pumped gas, fixed flats, and washed and waxed vehicles. At the time I graduated, I was not able to get on with the U.S. Forest Service because their yearly budget (including money for new employees) was not approved until October. Meanwhile, I had several cousins working for the Forest Service who were keeping an eye out for me. After I finished up for the day at the gas station, I'd walk across the street to Twitty's Restaurant and wash dishes until ten or eleven at night. Leon Adickes and Dr. Grover Winslow, two Hemphill businessmen, had built the restaurant several years earlier. They named it after the country singer, Conway Twitty, who came to town for the grand opening spring of 1971. I can still remember him arriving in a red and white Cadillac and doing a live concert on a flatbed float in front of the restaurant. I was still working at the Conoco Station when I finally got the word that the U.S. Forest Service had three openings. My hiring on December 10th, 1973, marked the beginning of my 36-year career (including the time I worked there while in high school) as an employee of the Forest Service.

From what I have shared with you, it probably sounds like I spent most of my childhood and teen years working. In fact, that is exactly what I did. My lack of a stable home life is probably one of the reasons I stayed busy all the time; that as well as being the breadwinner for my mama and sister. I didn't develop hobbies as a young person because there wasn't time or money for those kinds of things. Instead, I developed a good sense of humor and a wealth of stories to share with others.

Before I begin to focus on the second chapter of my life, I do want to share some of the experiences that involved my mama. Though most of what I learned during my childhood came from men in the community and male relatives, I have her to thank for some of the knowledge I gained related to cooking and household chores.

From watching my mama, I developed my barbecuing techniques. She'd take the meat and season it with salt and pepper before putting it on the pit. She made her own barbecue sauce and though she never wrote down the recipe, my wife and I have found that we can create the same taste, using a store-bought barbecue sauce and adding ingredients to spice it up. Mama created what she called a "barbecue mop" from a forked stick and a piece of sheet. After starting the meat, she would periodically turn it, using the mop to baste it with a mixture of butter, liquid hickory, and vinegar. Once the meat was tender, she would apply the barbecue sauce as a glaze on both sides of the meat. Through trial-and-error, I combined her techniques with some of my own in order to prepare what others tell me are "mouth-watering" ribs, chicken, and brisket.

Mama taught me how to make beef tripe and chitlins, usually cooked during the holidays when I was growing up. Today, this is still a family tradition for us. When I was a youngster, you could get beef stomach lining (tripe) and pig intestines, used for chitlins, at a meat locker or slaughter house. You didn't have to pay anything for those animal parts. To clean tripe, you soaked it overnight in vinegar and salt water until it turned white. Then you cut it up in small blocks, adding Creole seasoning, onions, and garlic and boiling it until tender. Today, our favorite way to prepare it is to first dip it in buttermilk, and then a mixture of ¾ cup of corn meal and ¼ cup of flour before deep fat frying it until golden brown. I hope my grandchildren will develop a taste for these traditional holiday foods as my children did.

Though I helped my mom make hog head cheese when I was younger, she later made sure my wife also knew her process for doing it. Like the barbecue sauce, she didn't have a written recipe to follow. Mama always put the hog head, ears, and feet in the pot. Deboning the meat after it was boiled was time consuming because pig feet have so many bones. We decided to try it without the feet, and the end result was just as tasty. I think my mama added the feet to make the parts of the pig go as far as possible. What I find interesting is the fact that the animal products used to make tripe, chitlins, and hog head cheese used to be "throw-away" parts. Today, these same parts are as expensive as most cuts of meat.

A neighbor raised corn, and he stored the ears in a corncrib. When my mama would get hungry for hominy, she'd send me down to his place, and I would climb into the crib and bring back 25-28 ears of corn. Using one cob against another, we'd rub the corn off the cobs. Then we would boil the corn in a cooking pot filled with water and lye. After a lot of rinsing, which is the secret to getting rid of the lye, we'd have delicious hominy to eat.

After our experience with trying to raise our own pig for slaughter, my mama started buying hogs from Austin Edgar, a local farmer who raised them to sell. In the summer, Edgar came through the community with a jeep full of fresh vegetables for sale. If he had meat to sell, he'd drive a pickup truck with a freezer full of ice in the back. We bought our pig during the winter when we could keep the meat for a longer period of time. After butchering it, we'd put the skin and fat in a washpot and cook it over a fire to get cracklins and lard. With the hog lard, my mama would make lye soap. She'd put it in a large loaf pan and let it harden. Then she'd cut it into blocks for us to use on laundry days.

When I was a kid, washday involved a whole lot more work than the way we do it now. I had four pots to fill with water before we could even start. A fire was necessary if Mama intended to wash white clothes. First, she would set a washpot full of water on the fire and then add the white clothes and a bar of lye soap. Those clothes came out snow white! The colored clothes were put in a #3 washpot with some washing powder. We'd use a rub board to get any stains out of the clothing. Then there were two pots full of clean water for rinsing all the clothes before you rolled up each item and squeezed hard to remove the water. The more water you got out, the faster the clothes would dry. We hung the clothes up with clothespins on a rope line in the yard. If I wanted to stiffen my jeans, I would have to mix starch with water and dunk my jeans in the mixture before hanging them up to dry. This is the way we did our laundry until I was fourteen or fifteen years old. When a washateria opened up nearby, we started using their gas washers and dryers to clean our clothes. We'd carry our dirty clothes there, tied up in a sheet, and be finished much faster than when we did the wash by hand. Today, I have two washpots that hang as planters in my front yard – one is my mama's and the other was used by an aunt. They help remind me of how hard it used to be to do the wash.

As I conclude this section of my autobiography, I'm inserting some favorite family recipes, including the Hog Head Cheese recipe Fay and I developed after helping my mama make it.

Hog Head Cheese Recipe

2 medium hog heads
¾ cup salt
½ cup black pepper
¼-½ cup red pepper (depending on your taste)
¼ cup garlic (cloves)
1 whole onion, peeled
6-8 bay leaves

Prior to cooking the hog heads, cut each head into fourths. Wash thoroughly with water. Then soak overnight in salty water. Rinse well before cooking. Put the heads in a huge pot. Cover with water. Add the rest of the ingredients. Stir frequently; add hot water as it cooks down. Once meat starts to get tender, taste a small piece to determine if more seasoning is needed. Do this periodically and season accordingly. Cook until meat starts to fall off bone (remove as many bones as possible while cooking). Once meat is tender, remove all meat from the pot and put in a large container to cool down. Be sure to save some broth to use later. Wearing plastic gloves, remove all fine bones from the cooled meat. Season deboned meat with:

½-¾ cup sage
2-4 tsp. red pepper flakes
½–¾ cup white vinegar

Mix the above ingredients into the meat while still wearing the gloves. Use a meat grinder (coarse blade) and feed all the meat through it. Once the meat is ground, taste again to determine if you need more seasoning (salt, pepper, etc.) Add enough reserved broth to slightly moisten meat in order to be able to press it into a crock bowl. Leave enough space between the meat and the top of the crock to allow you to place a dinner plate over the meat. Place something heavy on the plate (ie; large can of pork/beans) to press it down. Refrigerate overnight. Once the meat jells, remove the plate and slice as needed.

Cajun Creole Peas

1 quart fresh or frozen purple hull or black-eye peas
½ pound of ham chunks or about six slices of bacon
1 pound of your favorite smoked sausage
small to medium onion, diced
1 tsp. minced garlic
1-10 oz. can of mild or original Rotel tomatoes
(or substitute can of diced or stewed tomatoes)
1-8 oz. can of tomato sauce
about 2 tsp. of salt (season to taste)
about 6 pods of small whole okra (optional)

Add a small amount of cooking oil to 4-6 quart pot. Put in ham chunks or bacon, cut into small pieces. Cut smoked sausage into rounds and add to pot. Cook until slightly browned; add diced onion and garlic and continue to cook until onion is wilted. Add remaining ingredients (except peas and okra); mix well. Gently stir in peas until mixed well with other ingredients. Cover all ingredients with hot water and stir to combine them. Boil for about an hour or until peas are tender. Add more water as needed and taste for seasoning. Add okra the last 15-20 minutes of cooking. Serve over white fluffy rice with cornbread.

Syrup Teacakes

4 cups all-purpose sifted flour
2 cups sugar
1 cup syrup
1 cup butter
1 cup butter-flavored Crisco shortening
1 tsp. baking soda
3 tsp. baking powder
½ cup buttermilk
3 eggs
1½ tsp. cinnamon
1 tsp. each: nutmeg, allspice, ginger

In a large bowl, mix shortening and butter until creamy. Add sugar and syrup; mix well. Beat eggs into mixture, one at a time. Stir baking powder and spices into flour; stir baking soda into buttermilk. Add flour, alternately with buttermilk, to other ingredients. Beat until blended. Put batter into refrigerator until chilled. Sprinkle flour onto pastry cloth and knead into batter. On a lightly floured pastry cloth, use rolling pin and roll out ⅓ of batter about ¼ inch thick. Use rim of a medium size drinking glass to cut cookies. Another option: Once batter has chilled, knead enough flour into batter to prevent sticking to hands; then estimate an amount that will cover a 9x13-inch cookie sheet and press it onto the ungreased cookie sheet. Bake at 350 degrees for 10-12 minutes or until cookies are lightly brown. Watch carefully and don't overcook. When cookies are done, cut into small equal squares. Place cookies in a large container, and while still hot, lay slices of white bread on top of them. When all cookies are baked and cooled, take bread out and cookies will remain soft and moist.

—Louella Dupree Holmes' original recipe

Mackerel or Salmon Croquettes

1 can Chicken of the Sea mackerel or pink salmon (or your favorite brand)
salt and pepper to taste
½ cup chopped onion
1 small seeded jalapeno, chopped (optional)
1 egg
2 heaping tbsp. cornmeal
about ⅓ cup canned evaporated milk (to moisten)

Drain mackerel or salmon* and place in medium size mixing bowl. Take out small bones and flake fish. Add small amount of salt and pepper (fish contains salt). Stir in chopped onion and jalapeno. Beat egg with milk and add to mixture. tir in cornmeal and more milk, if needed, to moisten mixture. Spoon patties or roll in cracker crumbs and drop into hot oil. Fry until golden brown on both sides. Drain on paper towel.

*Broth that is poured off fish can be used to make gravy. Brown 2 tbsp. of flour in 2 tbsp. of oil fish was fried in. Add about 2 tbsp. of minced onion to flour mixture. Add enough water to broth to make two cups of liquid. Whisk broth into flour mixture, add salt and pepper to taste, and cook over medium heat until desired thickness.

—Croquettes Recipe: Gloria Fay Holmes; Gravy: Louella Dupree Holmes

My wife, Fay, developed the following recipe after watching my mama (Louella Dupree Holmes) make chicken and dumplings. The measurements are not exact because my mama didn't have a written recipe.

Chicken and Dumplings

1 seasoned whole hen, fryer, or chicken parts
salt and pepper to taste
1 stalk of celery, cut into chunks
1 small onion, cut into chunks
1 tsp. Wyler's chicken bouillon granules or cubes for each cup of water
(if desired)
2-4 quarts of chicken broth from chicken
2-3 cups all-purpose flour
1 tbsp. butter-flavored Crisco to each cup of flour
ice water
about 1 cup of canned evaporated milk (Pet or Carnation)

Season chicken lightly because bouillon contains salt. Put the chicken in a large pot and cover with water. Add celery, onion, and bouillon; boil until tender. As chicken cooks, occasionally taste broth for seasoning. After chicken is done, remove from broth and debone. Discard celery and onion, but keep broth. Sift together flour and salt. Make a mound of flour in the center of the mixing bowl in the same way you would prepare homemade biscuits. Cut Crisco into the mound of flour with a fork until particles are fine. Use a fork to blend in enough ice water with flour to make a smooth batter. Use a mixing spoon and continue to blend; then mix in extra flour until dough forms a ball. Chill dough for a few hours. Divide dough, roll thin, and cut into strips about 1½ inches wide. Bring broth to a rolling boil (if needed, add about 2 tbsp. of butter to broth to enhance richness). Drop dumpling strips into boiling broth, a few at a time, and stir lightly to keep separated. After all are in broth, cover and simmer for about 30 minutes (continue to stir gently so dumplings won't stick). Add extra broth if needed; dumplings need to have a generous amount of gravy when done. Add chicken and about one cup of canned evaporated milk to dumplings to make a creamy gravy. Stir very lightly and serve.

Syrup Bread

1 cup Ribbon Cane Syrup
1 cup sugar
2 cups sifted all-purpose flour
1 cup vegetable oil
1 cup buttermilk
2 eggs
1 tsp. baking soda
pinch of salt
1 tsp. each: cinnamon, nutmeg, ginger, and allspice

Mix vegetable oil, sugar, and eggs; stir baking soda, salt and spices into flour. Add flour, alternately with buttermilk, to oil mixture. Beat on medium speed until blended. Spray non-stick cooking spray or Baker's Joy in a 9x13-inch pan. Pour batter in and bake at 350 degrees for 30-45 minutes. Do the toothpick test to see if bread is done.

—Original Recipe of: Louella Dupree Holmes

Here I am with Laila, my granddaughter.
I look forward to passing on our family recipes to
her and her brother, Kobe.

Dirty Rice Dressing

1 pound ground chuck
1 pound chicken gizzards
½ pound chicken livers
1 cup rice
chicken broth
1 stick of butter
1 cup chopped onion
1 clove minced garlic
½ cup chopped bell pepper
½ cup chopped celery
pinch of thyme and sweet basil
1 bunch green onion tops, finely chopped
1 tbsp. minced parsley
salt and pepper to taste
Tony Chachere's Seasoning – to taste (optional)
red pepper flakes (season to taste)

Cook rice in chicken broth until fluffy. Cover gizzards and livers with water; add chicken bouillon or granules according to amount of water. Season lightly with salt and pepper because bouillon also contains salt. Drop in a few pieces of celery and onion to enhance the flavor of the broth. Take livers out when tender and continue to cook gizzards. Add extra water as needed. In a large skillet, sauté ground beef until all pink is gone. Drain any excess grease and discard. When giblets are tender and cool, chop fine with food processor (reserve juice from giblets); add to ground beef along with one stick of butter and brown. Season well with salt and pepper. Add juice from giblets to meat mixture. Sauté all vegetables in about 1 tbsp. of butter; add to meat mixture and continue to simmer for about ten additional minutes. Taste before combining all ingredients with cooked rice. Spoon into a large pan and mix well. If too dry, add extra chicken broth. After mixing thoroughly, taste for seasoning. Place rice dressing in a large baking dish and cover with foil. Place in 250 degrees oven and heat thoroughly, about 20-30 minutes, until steaming hot. The secret of this dressing is to keep all ingredients moist at all stages of cooking. Recipe can be doubled if desired.

—Recipe from: Gloria Fay Holmes

This is a photograph of me from the 1960-61 Thomas Johnson School Annual.
(I was in the first grade.)

SECTION TWO: ADULTHOOD

When I was hired as a forestry technician by the U.S. Forest Service on December 10, 1973, I felt like I was starting a new chapter in my life. For the first time, I had a job with good benefits and the opportunity for pay advancements if I was willing to apply myself. Unlike many people who can hardly wait to grow up so they can move away from home, I loved the place where I had grown up and intended to stay there, but I also wanted to have a wife and raise children in the community I had lived in all my life. The problem was most jobs available in this part of Texas barely paid enough to get by, let alone allowed you to provide a comfortable life for a family. As a Forest Service employee, I was starting out at $3.36 per hour, and I was determined to do whatever it took to increase my take-home pay.

The crew at the Yellowpine Work Center
(I'm third from the right leaning on the sign)

Starting in December, which marks the beginning of the tree planting season for the Forest Service, meant that is what I did until late February. Early in March and through part of April, I did what is called TSI (Timber Stand Improvement), which involves thinning the forest to allow better growth for the remaining trees. From late April through November, I worked recreation and maintained the land lines identifying U.S. government land. I cleared brush to establish a sight line for the markings we placed on trees to show where the boundaries were. Red "X's" were painted on trees and we blazed the line: four hacks on the tree identified government land; three hacks identified private land.

Working recreation meant I could be doing any or all of the following jobs at one of the U.S. recreation areas the Yellowpine Work Center was responsible for: mowing, raking, cleaning bathrooms, picking up trash, and painting and maintaining signs for park visitors. Indian Mounds, Red Hill Lake, Willow Oak, and Lakeview Campground were the four recreation areas our work center maintained.

Nine months after I was hired by the Forest Service, I started dating my future wife, Gloria Fay Mosley (I have always called her by her middle name). I first met her when I was ten and she was eight years old. She used to spend time at Joe Dupree's house because Fay's mother was married to my cousin at that time. Fay actually lived in San Augustine with her grandmother, who was raising her, but often visited her mom. We'd play together while she was next-door, and I can remember times when Joe and her mom would take us to the fairs and carnivals held in Center, Texas. After Joe and Fay's mom separated, we lost contact with each other.

Ten years later, we ran into each other at a small fair in San Augustine. We visited briefly, and then went our separate ways. I guess she still wanted to give me that kiss she had tried to give me back when I was ten years old because the next thing I knew, my cousin, Betty Jenkins, was relaying a message that Gloria wanted me to call her. Betty lived in the Black Ankle Community and had been several years ahead of Fay in high school. One Sunday evening, instead of calling her, I drove over to where I thought Fay lived and found her and her cousin walking on the road – one of the things kids did back then. I turned my car around, and we struck up a conversation.

Soon after, we started dating; it was September 1974. On our first official date, I picked her up in my 1968 golden brown Fairlane Ford and brought her to Hemphill to see my mama. I had purchased this car when I gave Mama my 1965 Ford to drive. Fay's mom, Louise, and my mama had been good friends when Louise was married to Joe, so my mama already knew Gloria Fay though she hadn't seen her for a long time. It didn't take me long to decide I wanted to marry Fay. Her response, however, wasn't as enthusiastic as I had hoped it would be. She was worried about her grandmother, a severe diabetic, and she wasn't sure she should move away from her. Fay's grandma had been hospitalized shortly after we started dating and though back at home, she needed an insulin injection each day. Fay had been the one giving her the shot. I tried to convince Fay we could still get married, promising I would drive her to San Augustine each day to give her grandmother the shot. That's exactly what happened once we were married – a daily trip to her grandmother's until Fay was able to train a younger cousin living there to do the injections.

When "smooth-talking" finally won Fay over, we tied the knot on December 20, 1974. I had $25 to last me until my next paycheck. I used ten dollars for the blood test, ten dollars for the license, and I paid Justice of the Peace Schulze five dollars to marry us. We had told my mom and Fay's grandmother that we intended to get married in Hemphill. I had hung some cans on the rear bumper and sprayed "Just Married" on the windows. After getting the marriage certificate, I circled the Hemphill ISD parking lot and then drove through East Mayfield, a section of Hemphill where I had relatives living, to show off my beautiful bride. We were poor folks so that was the extent of our celebrating. In fact, we were going to start out our married life living with my mother. That wasn't a good situation for Fay because my mama did not want to share her only son with any other woman. In fact, the first thing she demanded to see after our marriage was the certificate – if we didn't have proof we were married, as far as she was concerned, we couldn't live together in her house.

My mama (Louella Dupree Holmes)

We lived with my mama for a little over two years before we were able to move into our own home and to this day, I deeply appreciate what my wife put up with while living with my mother. There was no way Mama was going to believe any woman could make her son happy, and she made that very clear to Fay. My wife proved her wrong time and again. As I turn 60, we are also celebrating our 40th wedding anniversary later in the year. I had expected my marriage to last a lifetime, and we're well on our way to accomplishing that goal.

When I married Fay, she had a ten-month-old son named Cedric. Fay's grandma wanted to keep him with her, but I insisted he was going to be part of our family, and I was going to be his daddy. Early in our marriage, Fay was working at Frontier Park on weekends, so I would babysit Cedric. After trying to wean Cedric off a pacifier with little success, I put hot sauce on it. It worked, though Fay couldn't initially figure out why he'd say, "hot, hot" from then on whenever he would see the pacifier. Just like my daddy before me, I would stick Cedric in the car on the seat next to me, and he was content to ride around all day. I loved playing jokes on him. Coming home late one night, I got the notion to tie his feet to the bed with some twine. I knew for sure when he woke up because he started hollering, "Mama, Mama, someone broke into our house and tied me up!"

On February 23, 1977, our first daughter was born in Nacogdoches, Texas, at Memorial Hospital, the same hospital in which I was born. The day Christunya Tashay was born, I was in the process of getting a house moved on to property next to my mama's house. With the arrival of a second child, we needed a place of our own. Fay went into labor the evening of February 22, and I took her to the hospital and stayed with her until midnight. The doctor wasn't sure when Tashay would be born and since I knew I had to prepare the house to be moved, I drove the 65 miles back to Hemphill that night. Tashay was born at 2:42 a.m., several hours after I had headed home. After jacking up the house and getting it ready to move, I drove back to Nacogdoches, anxious to welcome my baby girl to this world. I was able to bring Fay home after three days in the hospital, but we had to leave Tashay there for two weeks because she had infant jaundice and a kidney infection. I'd go to work during the day; then we'd drive to the hospital each night to see Tashay.

The house that was being moved while Fay was in the hospital had originally been sitting on property on County Road 944. I had purchased it from Norman Hoyt for $500. We had agreed on that price after he told me I could have it for what it would cost him to purchase a bathtub, commode, and bathroom sink. I went to Leslo's Lumber Yard in Hemphill, priced those items, and found that they would cost $500. With the purchase price settled, I hired Glen Coon, a house mover in San Augustine, to move the house to my property for $900. That happened on February 24, 1977. I was working with a $2,000 bank loan – the rest of the money went to pour concrete for the front porch which allowed us to step up into the house.

The whole experience involved in obtaining a loan for a house and then paying it off taught me a costly but important lesson. I am sure it prevented me from making similar mistakes in the future as well as ultimately saving me money. There are so many experiences in my life that molded and shaped me into the person I am today. When I secured my loan, I had operated on the assumption that although I was signing a contract, I didn't have to worry about reading it in detail because the banker had told me he had known my daddy and had no problem with giving me a loan. Several years into making my monthly payments (we kept the receipts in a Panama Royal Cigar box), I had someone familiar with legal language read my loan contract and inform me I had made a grave mistake in signing the contract without knowing all the details in it. I worked hard to pay off that loan but resolved to never sign another legal document unless an attorney looked at it. I also decided to avoid purchasing items where a loan was involved, though that same banker was anxious to give me a home improvement loan. Instead, I saved and made do until I had the cash to make my purchase. Now I think of all the money I put back in my own pocket because I wasn't paying interest to someone else. Car loans were my exception, since it's difficult to "make do" without a vehicle.

After Tashay was born, we still had to live with my mama until I was able to get some things done on the house. The first time Fay saw it she was not a bit impressed, although I assured her it had good bones. I had contacted Truitt "Shorty" Little, a carpenter, about sealing the house. Someone had suggested I contact him after hearing what Mr. Coon, the house mover, wanted to charge me for doing it. Shorty's fee was half the amount I had been quoted by Mr. Coon. I'd work at the Forest Service during the day and spend the night working on the house. I was averaging two-three hours of sleep per night, but I was determined to provide my family with their own home as soon as possible. Initially I ran a water line from my cousin's house until I was able to dig a well on my property. My first improvement to the house was to replace the tin roof with plywood that I covered with shingles. When we moved in, the only furniture we had was what Norman Hoyt had left in the house when he sold it to me. Although we had a bathroom, I had to install a septic system before it was useable.

Our home has been a work in progress for 37 years. I have added onto the original house several times, replaced the shingle roof with a metal one, totally remodeled the kitchen, added granite countertops, replaced flooring, and the list goes on. Through it all, each project was done after I had either saved enough money to purchase the supplies and pay all other costs, or I had worked on a job for Shorty Little and in return he assisted me with one of my remodeling projects. Shorty and I had become close friends over the years. If I worked for him in the evenings, he would help me at my house on weekends. He'd give me left-over materials from a job if he thought I could use them. I can remember Cedric, as a young child, climbing over lumber I had stored in his bedroom for the next home improvement project.

What our house looked like prior to the improvements.
Notice the old washpots hanging in our front yard.

Our house in 2014

The first time Tashay got sick she was still a baby. When we took her to the doctor, he gave us a prescription for amoxicillin and cough syrup. I didn't have enough money to pay for the whole prescription when I went to get it filled at the Hemphill Drug Store, so I asked the pharmacist, Jim Olive, if I could buy just half of it. He told me he couldn't do that since it was a medication he had to mix up. What he offered to do, instead, was to allow me to have the medicine and pay him later. What he asked in return was that I did repay him, instead of ignoring it and slipping off somewhere else to get another prescription filled. He said even if all I had was a penny to apply to my bill, he would continue to fill my prescriptions as long as I made the effort to pay on my charge. He accepted my word that I would repay him, and that is exactly what I did as quickly as I could. In return, I earned his trust. From that point on, Fay or I could give him a call, pick up needed medicine for the kids, and know he would charge it until we had the money to pay him back. Several times when we couldn't afford to see a doctor, he assisted us with information on over-the-counter medicines that made our children well. He was a role model for Tashay and encouraged her to attend pharmacy school. Jim Olive added to my collection of "life" lessons: honor your word and never shrink from your debt, regardless of circumstances; you were extended a courtesy, so repay it as soon as possible.

After five years as a forestry technician, I transferred to a road and firefighting crew. Prior to the move, I had to get a commercial driver's license (CDL) because the job involved working with dump trucks and other pieces of heavy equipment. I also had to take a Step Test which amounted to exactly what the title suggests: stepping up and down on a box for 30 minutes and then having your pulse checked. The purpose of the test was to determine if you were fit enough to fight forest fires. It wasn't uncommon for one of your friends to "pick at you" during the test in an attempt to make you lose your concentration so you had to start over. The Step Test was a yearly test and up to the age of 53 (when I retired), I had never failed it. With the move to this position, my pay doubled which assisted me greatly in providing for my family.

Our young family: Tashay, Cedric, Fay and myself

As part of a U.S. Forest Service firefighting crew, I could be sent to any part of the United States to fight forest fires on national land. The first time I was sent off, I went to Eureka, California, for twelve days. As part of a hand crew, I constructed fire lines up the mountainside to control the fire. Using rakes and shovels, our 20-man crew dug out a two-foot line to help halt the fire. We dealt with steep terrain, the possibility of rock slides, and burning tree snags. We often were fighting at night when the wind died down, and we could control the fire more effectively. Cutting a tree while it is burning is an "on the edge" experience. Over the years, I fought wildfires in Idaho, West Virginia, Virginia, Louisiana, North and South Carolina, Florida, New Mexico, Oregon, Nevada, Utah, and, of course, Texas. Along with a hazardous job came hazard pay. Sometimes, however, the hazards had nothing to do with the fire. I was part of a three-man crew digging a fire line with a rake in Virginia's Shenandoah National Park, when I happened to look up and see a big black bear ahead of me. As I managed to croak out the word "BEAR," I realized the other two guys were out of sight behind me. My second attempt to sound an alarm was louder and brought one of the guys running to see what was going on. He suggested that the candy in my pocket might be what the bear was after. I pulled that candy out of my pocket, tossed it toward the bear, and rapidly headed in the opposite direction. I never took another piece of candy with me while out on a fire.

In Idaho on the Salmon River

I had several experiences when on assignment to fight fires near McAllen, Texas, that gave my crew buddies something to laugh about. Don Eddings, a close friend and fellow Forest Service employee, and I had decided to cross the border into Mexico so I could buy Gucci purses for my wife and daughters. Someone had told me they were much cheaper in Mexico. Since it is against regulations to take government vehicles across the border, we parked our fire truck at a fast food place near the border and walked across into Mexico. Coming upon some pretty gross looking cooked meat being sold out of a big tub on the side of the street, I offered to buy Don his supper. While he was giving me a piece of his mind regarding my offer, I thought I heard someone calling my name. I looked around but didn't see anyone I recognized. The second time it happened we both heard it and realized it was a guy who had been working with us earlier fighting the fire. He had his car with him and offered us a ride back to our vehicle. At the border, I was the only one asked to produce identification. Neither Don nor the other guy had to dig out their license. When I asked what was going on, I was told I was the only one they were unsure of as far as race went. Although the guy driving was Hispanic, he crossed the border often and was known to them. Thereafter, I started noticing that when Don and I would go to a store, the clerk would speak to him in English and address me in Spanish. I guess my skin color was really confusing folks along the border.

I think Don and Greg Cohrs, another close friend and Forest Service employee from our work center, had the biggest laugh over the confusion about my race when we were heading home and had to stop at a checkpoint just out of McAllen. I was sitting in the front seat between Greg and Don and as we approached the checkpoint, we watched a bunch of guys climb out of the back of a vehicle in front of us and take off, trying to get around the border patrol agents without getting caught. When we pulled up to the agent checking the vehicles, Greg leaned out and after acknowledging the problem the agents were dealing with, remarked as he nodded toward me, "We've got one here we caught for you; he was just too fat to jump the fence." I guess you know that story got repeated a number of times.

Through the Forest Service, I received district fire training, including the use of dozers to put out wildfires and construct fire control lines. I also learned how to do bulldozer maintenance and repairs. I was still part of the road crew for my work center, so when not dealing with fire issues, I cleaned culverts, graded roads, did brush hogging and anything else necessary to maintain the forest service roads in recreation areas and national forest in Sabine County, Texas. Though I had a specific job description throughout my career with the

Forest Service, I was willing to do anything that needed to be done and, thus, acquired more skills as a result. I never recall saying, "that's not my job." We were on call 24 hours a day and, at times, worked long hours. One holiday weekend I was working at Willow Oak Park and just as I was ready to leave, I noticed a couple stalled on the side of the road with a broken fan belt. I drove up to Hemphill, called a guy I knew to open up a parts shop so I could get a fan belt, and then drove back to the park to install it for them. The couple expressed their appreciation and tried to pay me for assisting them, saying what a good fellow I was to help out complete strangers on a holiday. I refused to accept any money because that's not my nature. Several days later, I arrived at work to find an envelope waiting for me. In it, I found a note from the guy I had helped, along with fifty dollars in cash for my services.

Working long hours and being away fighting fires for days at a time meant my wife did a lot of the child-rearing. However, I took my duties as a dad seriously and was involved in my children's activities whenever I was home. If Fay had to leave for work before I did, I would take Cedric and Tashay to school. A cousin, Miss Shirley, would watch them in the cafeteria and make sure they got their breakfast. When Cedric mentioned to Shirley that he was still hungry after eating the food on his tray, I made sure she had additional money to get him an extra tray anytime he wanted one, telling her I never wanted my children to experience the hunger I had felt as a child.

Since I wanted my children to develop good character, I tended to utilize some of the same techniques used on me to teach them responsibility for their actions. Cedric liked to ride to the store with me because the owner always gave him a piece of candy. One day he decided to take a piece of candy on his own. When I discovered he had it, I took him back inside the store, made him return it, and then gave him a whipping on the spot. I never wanted Cedric to feel that taking something without permission was acceptable. I hoped that he had learned the same lesson Mr. Coolridge taught me after he caught me stealing from his garden.

Cedric with Tashay

Cedric and Tashay were our only children until Felondria was born ten years later. They both had specific chores because I wanted them to learn how to work and value the end result of their labor. Cedric was responsible for feeding some hogs we had, and Tashay fed our rabbits. Cedric took out the trash, and both children folded clothes. They took turns washing the dishes. Tashay actually started washing dishes when she was still small enough that she had to stand on a stool. I even had a contract they had to sign to get paid for their chores. During the summer, I took Cedric with me when I was hauling watermelons or hay. Both kids picked blueberries at Winslow's Farm, and Cedric picked peas at Julius Smith's Farm with a group of boys his age. The job they complained about the most was hand mowing the yard. Fay was convinced I was going to kill them in the heat, but I had noticed how quickly they "revived" every time they took a break - they seemed to have plenty of energy for playing.

I value education because, aside from a good work ethic, it provides young people with the best opportunity to succeed in today's world. I speak from experience, wishing now that I had been better able to take advantage of what my teachers were trying to do for me. To demonstrate to my children the importance I attached to a good education, I made sure I attended their "Open Houses" and all other school functions, provided I was not away on a job. Many times I would come in from working overtime, clean up, and then head to Hemphill to a school activity, especially when they were in high school. I called it "parent police patrol" – checking to make sure my kids were doing what they said they were going to do on any given evening. I expected them to show respect for their teachers and make the most of their time in the classroom. It was my habit to periodically pay their teachers a visit, so I could check on them. They always tried to get me to tell them when I intended to drop by the school, but that was "classified" information. Fay and I were giving them the kind of home life I had missed out on, so they could be focused in the classroom and benefit from what they were being taught. To motivate my children to do their best, I gave them two dollars for each "A" and one dollar for each "B" on their report cards. If one of them received a low grade, rather than punish them for it, I simply encouraged that child to do better next time. I didn't want to place so much emphasis on grades that they began to dislike or fear school.

Tashay was very self-motivated and set high standards for herself, both in the classroom and in sports. When she was little, she played for the Red Sox Team in the local Dixie League. I attended many of her games and had told her I expected good sportsmanship from her at all times because I knew how competitive she was. I'm sure it took great restraint on her part, but she never "showed out." I still have the little red glove she used while playing ball.

I had a red 1966 Ford pickup sitting in the backyard that Tashay and Cedric decided to take for a "joy ride" down in the pasture one day while Fay and I were gone. When we returned and they saw me standing in the yard, the two of them sat in that truck out in the middle of the pasture, crying and carrying on, convinced they were going to get the whipping of their lives. I told them if they could get that truck back up to the house, there would be no whipping. You should have seen the determination on their faces as Tashay slowly but surely popped that clutch in and out, and they inched their way back up to the yard.

I wasn't likely to repeat a request to my children too many times. One morning it dawned on me that Tashay had developed the habit of expecting me to call her several times before she would get out of bed on school days. So that particular morning, I didn't repeat the request when she failed to get up - I simply left her in the bed. When she finally did get up and realize she had missed a major test, Tashay really carried on but never missed a "wake-up" call after that.

When Cedric was eleven years old, we had a real scare with him. It began with an imaginary telephone conversation with someone who wasn't there. Realizing he was hallucinating, we took him to our local doctor who promptly admitted him to the hospital in Hemphill. We knew he had recently bumped his leg on a chain link fence, but what we didn't know was the fact that he had developed osteomyelitis, an infection and inflammation of the bone. After he had been hospitalized locally for twenty-one days with no improvement, I made the decision to move him to a larger hospital. Dr. McLean in Nacogdoches, Texas, immediately diagnosed the problem and operated on him to clean out the wound in his leg bone. Between the two hospitals, it was almost two months before he was able to come home. It was difficult for us to have one of our children away from home, so we tried to be at the hospital as much as our jobs would allow. I could take more time off during the week than Fay's job allowed; weekends we both could be with him. He required two additional surgeries with hospital stays of one week each to scrape the infection from the bone. Between his surgeries, we cared for the wound ourselves. It was almost two years before he was completely healed.

You can see the scar on Cedric's leg in this photo.

Fay was a paraprofessional at Brookeland I.S.D, when she started working on a degree in elementary education in 1984. I had promised Fay's granddad before he died that I would make sure she got a college degree. Shortly before I convinced her to get married, he had been preparing to assist her with the admission process at Stephen F. Austin State University. Though both he and his wife came to trust me when they saw I was taking good care of their granddaughter, he initially had not been in favor of our marriage. Fay's granddad had his heart set on her going to college, and he had been setting money aside for that purpose.

When Fay began taking classes through Angelina College, Tashay, as a thirteen year old, started taking evening classes for college credit at the same time. At first, both of them had classes in Jasper, Texas, and I would take them. I'd wait for them in the car, catching up on my sleep until they were finished. Later Fay started car-pooling with a neighbor, and Tashay learned to drive so she could go on her own as long as it was daylight. In the winter, I would still do the driving because I didn't want her on the road by herself after dark. With the extra classes she took, Tashay entered college as a sophomore.

Our second daughter was born on September 29, 1986, in Memorial Hospital in Lufkin, Texas. Fay's cousin suggested we name her Felondria, a combination of both of our first names. When she was born, she was fair-skinned. I was rather startled, while watching her in the hospital nursery, to have a white woman walk up to the glass and claim Felondria as hers, saying, "That's my granddaughter." When I informed her the baby being pointed out belonged to me, the look of disbelief on her face led me to suggest she might want to look at the name on the child's crib. Several years later, we had a man stop us as Fay, Felondria, and I were walking into the Walmart in Jasper, Texas. After establishing the fact that we were the natural parents of Felondria, he wanted to know what race I was. "What race do you want me in?" was my first response, though I knew what he was trying to figure out. I told him I wasn't sure what race I was because my daddy was black and my mama was French.

Six weeks after Felondria was born, Fay had to return to her job at Brookeland I.S.D. An elderly neighbor across the road from us kept children, and she agreed to watch Felondria. Our youngest daughter soon became "Aunt" Ben's favorite. After she had Felondria for a while, she refused to take care of any other children. I was paying Aunt Ben $25 per week. When I discovered she was using that entire amount to buy what she called "wholesome" food for Felondria, I tried to pay her extra for the food, but she refused to accept it. Aunt Ben didn't believe in store-bought baby food and fed Felondria only home-cooked meals. Aunt Ben also had no use for Pampers; she was convinced they caused diaper rash. Instead, she put cloth diapers on Felondria, and she made sure she was the one who washed them. It wasn't uncommon for Aunt Ben to walk over on the weekend and when leaving, say to Felondria, "C'mon baby" and Felondria would obediently follow her back home. Aunt Ben kept Felondria for three years until she started daycare.

Felondria, almost ten years younger than Tashay, was a small bundle of extraordinary wisdom and common sense. Even Cedric and Tashay would ask her for advice. Felondria loved to be pushed on a yellow swing I had hung up in the yard. As she swung toward me, I would tickle her feet, and she'd shriek, "Do it again, Daddy!" I usually tired of the game before she did. Now I swing my grandkids on that same yellow swing, and Laila, if pushed too high calls out, "I'm scared! I'm scared." Things came easily to Felondria; she didn't have to put much effort into getting good grades or learning something new. Fay taught her to read by the age of three, and she soon had her own library.

While Tashay was more apt to be involved in outdoor activities, Felondria was a very girly girl though she did participate in the East Texas "Get Hooked on Fishing Not Drugs" event one year at Harborlight Marina on Toledo Bend Lake. Paul Hinton, an outdoor writer, had begun this youth anti-drug and alcohol abuse program about eight years earlier. I made an appearance as Smokey the Bear on behalf of the Forest Service and then changed out of the costume to help with the assorted activities planned for the day. Felondria caught her first fish and received a certificate and small prize.

Felondria reading at the age of three; her yellow swing is to the right.

Felondria with her first fish

As a five year old, Felondria loved to sing and dance. I bought her a toy microphone for Christmas, and we videotaped a tiny James Brown impersonator singing "I Feel Good" while imitating his best moves. She'd jump up, shuffle her feet, and do the splits (reminded me of myself dancing at Harvey's Café when I was a kid).

I recall one shopping experience with my three children that got me into hot water with Fay, primarily because nothing seemed to get past Felondria. We were at the mall in Lufkin trying to buy Fay a Mother's Day gift at Bealls. Felondria was quite small at the time. I was trying to get some information from the clerk who couldn't seem to understand me. When she started getting rude, I decided I had had enough and said, "I'm so sorry, ma'am, but my mama dropped me on my head when I was little and messed me up." The shocked look on her face was followed by an attitude adjustment, and I was treated politely from that point on. The first thing Felondria did when she saw Fay was to repeat what I had told the clerk. I know Fay wasn't happy about that, but sometimes hauling three kids around in a store trying to buy a Mother's Day gift can test the patience of even a saint.

In November 1989, Fay's mom and grandmother died in a house fire. As I watched her grieve, I thought about my promise to her grandfather regarding a college education for her. Though she had been attending night classes since 1984, I decided it was time for her to finish her education. With a job and family, she had been limited to taking one class per semester. I felt we needed her out of college before Tashay started. I didn't want to rely on any government loans, so I began working as much overtime as possible. I started looking at ways to increase my salary, knowing that I had a wife and two daughters to put through college. Cedric had already made it clear he wasn't interested in additional schooling after high school graduation. After Fay received an Associate of Science Degree from Angelina College on December 17, 1993, she transferred to Stephen F. Austin State University in Nacogdoches, Texas. For her last year of school, we decided it would be easier for her to live on campus. She'd come home those weekends when she didn't have projects or needed to study for a test. With Tashay helping, I felt I could take care of Felondria. The only time we ran into a problem was when Felondria needed her hair fixed for a special occasion, like school pictures. I solved that dilemma by putting her in the car around 4:00 a.m., while she was still sleeping, and taking her to Nacogdoches, so Fay could do her hair. Fay received her degree in elementary education on August 12, 1995, and the Monday after getting her degree, she was working as a special education/content mastery teacher for Brookeland I.S.D. (the same job she had been doing as an aide prior to getting her degree). Tashay graduated from high school spring of that same year.

Our family at Fay's graduation from college

During her sophomore year in high school, Tashay was playing basketball. A fierce competitor, she always pushed herself to do her best. She was also a member of the Hemphill High Steppers, her high school drill team. On one occasion, she ran into a scheduling conflict with basketball and drill team. Her basketball coach told her she would have to make a choice between the two. She chose the drill team, and I backed her on the decision. Days later several coaches showed up at the house and tried to talk me into having her rejoin the basketball team. We stuck by her initial choice and never regretted it. In place of basketball, she took up track the last two years in high school and won fifth in state her senior year. She ended up with a $75,000 track scholarship from Northwestern State University in Natchitoches. When Tashay, Gary Vanya (her high school track coach), and I visited the Northwestern campus prior to her starting college, I was very up front with their head coach. I told him we appreciated the scholarship and it was fine for her to run track, but I also had her there to do her academics and if her grades fell, she'd have to give up the scholarship and focus on her classes. After giving me a strange look, he told me I was the first parent he'd encountered who put academics first. After three years at Northwestern, Tashay transferred to the University of Houston where she earned her doctorate in pharmacy.

When Felondria reached high school, she was also on the drill team. Both Tashay and Felondria qualified for the American All-Stars Drill Team each year they competed which meant they were invited to perform nationally as well as in other countries. However, I wouldn't allow either of them to travel to most of the places where these events were held. I knew I couldn't take off work to go with them, and I was too protective to have them away on their own. I did give in on three occasions; Tashay got to go to London, and Felondria was able to go on two trips. In November 2002, Tashay had just finished college so she accompanied Felondria and the drill team on a Caribbean cruise. A year later, I sent all "three of my girls" to Hawaii, where Fay and Tashay got to watch Felondria perform with the All-Star Drill Team. I worked lots of overtime and did a number of fish fries in order to have the money for the trips. With my fund-raisers, I divided the money among all the girls from Hemphill who had qualified to make the trips.

Speaking of being protective, I earned a nickname from the teen boys when my girls reached the age where I would allow them to date. They called me "Reverend Bubba" because I was so strict. I didn't allow Tashay or Felondria to date until they were fifteen, and they had to be sixteen before they could go out in a car alone with a boy. When they were at the house with a boy, either Fay or myself had to be present. They couldn't go in their bedroom with the boy or cut off the lights in a room. It really irritated the girls when I started questioning one of their dates, and boys that disrespected the rules were told not to come back again. I'll agree I was strict, but I knew what was on the mind of most of those boys, and it wasn't what I wanted for my girls.

Once Tashay started driving, it was hard to slow her down. She drove like she ran – FAST! I dealt with several speeding tickets with her while she was attending Northwestern. When she got a ticket in Many, Louisiana, I went to the judge and asked him if there was any way we could avoid a speeding ticket. I told him she was in college, and I hated to have my car insurance go up. The judge took pity on me and reduced the ticket to a seatbelt infraction. Her next speeding ticket was issued in Natchitoches, Louisiana. Getting concerned about Tashay's driving, I called and discussed her speeding problem with the judge. Tashay wanted me to pay the ticket, but the judge advised me to make her appear in court. She was really nervous that day. After some typical "courtroom drama," she pleaded guilty to the speeding charge. Because she was in college, the judge gave her deferred adjudication for a year. He told her if she was caught speeding during that time, she would have both tickets on her record and be responsible for two fines; otherwise the ticket would be dismissed after a year. Before leaving the courtroom, the judge told her she needed to thank her daddy for being a good attorney for her. She still likes to speed, but I no longer have to deal with her tickets.

As I stated earlier, I place a high value on education because I think it helps prepare young people to be successful in the workplace. My goal was to assist my children in any way possible to get off to a good start in life once they left home. Both Tashay and Felondria went to college. Tashay earned her doctorate in pharmacy in 2002, and Felondria graduated in 2008 from Lamar University with a degree in Public Health Administration. Cedric wasn't interested in any schooling beyond high school. However, since I wanted him to have the best opportunity for success, I enlisted the help of a friend to get him a job with Temple Inland, a company with the opportunity for advancement if you worked hard. Wanting him to succeed at the job, I advised him to always be on time, do whatever he was asked to do, and perform the job to the best of his abilities. I knew his good manners would assist him in getting along with others.

In 1994, both the fleet manager and chain saw instructor for our forest district retired, and their duties passed on to me. I became responsible for inspecting, oiling, and maintaining all the vehicles and other pieces of equipment used at the Yellowpine Work Center, as well as issuing government driver licenses. Though I had been doing mechanic's work for many years, I received some specialized training through John Deere for some of our equipment. To assume the title of chain saw instructor, I had to attend classes and receive certification. I also had to have CPR training that I updated every three years. Along with the additional duties came a welcomed increase in pay. I continued to fight fires both within the district and off site, operate many pieces of equipment, and do whatever was asked of me. When sent to another state for a natural disaster at this point in my career, I was often assigned to be the fleet manager for the equipment being utilized.

There were three disasters that hit close to home and greatly affected me. When a monster El Nino passed through Shelby County to the north of Hemphill, Texas on February 10, 1998, I was assigned to maintain the fleet on-site during this incident. I couldn't believe the amount of damage. Timber was down everywhere; trees were tossed up in piles like toy Lincoln logs. As I operated a bull dozer trying to clear some of the roads in the area, I was struck by the "popcorn-like" sound the trees made as I pushed them aside. The storm had hit just as the kids were getting out of school, and many of them crawled over huge stacks of fallen trees to get to their homes. Amazingly, no lives were lost, although that was hard to believe when you looked at the amount of damage.

Taking a break after a day of cleaning up debris from El Nino

On February 1, 2003, when the Space Shuttle Columbia disintegrated over Texas and Louisiana and all seven astronauts were killed, Don Eddings and I were the first two Forest Service workers to report to the Yellowpine Work Center. At the beginning, we were assigned to the Search and Rescue Incident Team assembled by Marcus Beard, our district ranger. Forming a single-file line covering a quarter of a mile, we searched for the remains of the astronauts. That was our initial concern until all seven astronauts were found. Later, as search teams were brought in from NASA and wildland firefighters were dispatched here from other states to locate shuttle parts, I focused on keeping the U.S. Forest Service equipment being used in working condition and signing out the rental equipment we had brought in to assist with the recovery process. When Nathan Ener called and told us the shuttle nose cone had been spotted on Temple Inland property, I went out with Don Eddings and Tracy White (also a Forest Service employee) to cut down trees and build a bridge over a creek in order to bring the cone out of the woods.

Bringing out the shuttle nose cone (I'm on the far left)

Hurricane Rita hit Sabine County on September 23, 2005. Prior to the hurricane coming ashore along the Gulf, we had moved our equipment to the rodeo/fair grounds in Hemphill, Texas. After Rita passed through, I had to "cut" my way from my house to the fair grounds. Large trees, many torn up from the roots, were across the roads, making them impassable. As Forest Service personnel arrived, we took equipment out to start clearing the trees and debris off the roads. Many evacuees from the Houston/Beaumont Area had made it as far as Hemphill, where they were provided shelter in churches and other facilities. I had set up a shelter at Thomas Johnson School and had over 100 people sleeping there. After spending sixteen hours per day working for the Forest Service clearing trees, I was coming home to cook big pots of food for the people at Thomas Johnson School. Most of our area was without electricity for several weeks, and many homes had no water. FEMA came in with bottled water and food provisions. The National Guard and clean-up crews from other locations were housed at Hemphill ISD until all utilities were restored and school resumed. It took months to clean up the damage from this category 3 hurricane, the eye of which passed directly over Hemphill, Texas.

Though not classified as a disaster, the crash of a helicopter carrying United States Forest Service employees on March 10, 2005, was a factor in my decision to accept an early-out incentive offered by the government and retire on August 10, 2007. Charles Edgar, the Forest Service Fire Management Officer for Sabine National Forest, was killed in this crash along with two other individuals. We were doing a prescribed burn on national forest land near Shelbyville, Texas. Charles was in the helicopter, along with the pilot and a USFS Ignition Specialist. They were dropping plastic ignition spheres. I was on a bull dozer as they passed overhead. Minutes later, someone from the helicopter radioed, "Mayday, Mayday, we're going down!" I took off on the dozer toward the site of the crash and was the second one there. Michael Kay, a forestry technician out patrolling a line, arrived before me. Although the others were dead, Charles appeared to be breathing a little. The crash had set the woods on fire, so I pushed a fireline around the helicopter to prevent an explosion because it looked like fuel was leaking out of it. Charles was transported to the hospital in Center, Texas, where he was pronounced dead upon arrival. Charles, age 54, was one of the last few employees at my work enter who had been there about the same amount of time as me. It seemed like a sign that it was time for me to go.

Operating a 550 John Deere bulldozer

I had actually started thinking about early retirement when an early-out incentive had been offered the year I turned 50. The magic formula for the U.S. Forest Service was twenty years on the job and 50 years or older. Most of the guys I had worked with for years were gone, and I was having trouble with high blood pressure. However, I wanted to make sure I could afford to retire early. A good health insurance plan for both Fay and me as well as life insurance for me would be necessary before I could leave. When I was convinced I had those things covered, I waited for the next early-out incentive to be offered. Meantime, Charles was killed, and it really made me start thinking about wanting more time to spend with my family. I also wanted the opportunity to give back to the community some of what had been given to me over the years. Although I had always been involved in my community, the hours I spent working did not leave me a lot of time for civic activities. Thus, when the early-out incentive was again offered starting August 10, 2007, I immediately filled out my retirement paperwork. Our district ranger wanted me to continue to work for two additional years and had gotten permission to offer me a $13,000 raise if I would stay. In thinking about it, I decided the additional money would not buy me what I wanted - more family time and more time to be involved in my community. So in August 2007, I retired from the U.S. Forest Service. When you take the early-out incentive, you can't return to the job for three years. Shortly after three years had passed, I started getting calls about returning to work for the Forest Service. I keep so busy I don't possibly see how I would be able to fit in a fulltime job, though I must admit it is a good feeling to find out your skills/knowledge are still desired by your former employer.

My wife would probably tell you she sees little difference in my pre-and post-retirement life. I am up early in the morning and off and running before most retirees are awake. I am on the go all day, accomplishing as many tasks as I can. A short nap (while watching the 10:00 p.m. news) often refreshes me, and I'll be up half the night working on projects and problems I have on my mind. Although I have always been involved in my community, with my retirement, I found myself able to fulfill my desire to help improve the section of Texas I call home.

Prior to retirement, I had been president of the Macedonia Cemetery for four years. This cemetery has been the burial site for most of the black citizens of Sabine County for over a hundred years. Twice a year I scheduled a cleanup where those with relatives buried there were asked to show up and help; the rest of the time I maintained the grounds. Weldon McDaniel, Sabine County Historian, had contacted me prior to my retirement for assistance with several projects; after my retirement, he and I became more involved in locating cemeteries and updating cemetery records in our county. We updated the records for the Macedonia Cemetery. Mr. McDaniel located courthouse files that identified people buried in the cemetery whose names were not on the cemetery records. Talking to people familiar with the cemetery helped us to locate graves that weren't marked. Douglas Hamilton, a friend with folks buried at the cemetery, and I made crosses for these gravesites. However, there are still over a hundred folks buried there that have unmarked graves. In addition to finding, cleaning up, and fencing abandoned cemeteries on national forest land, we did the same thing for private cemeteries. We also put up a number of historical markers throughout the county.

In 2012, when the water level in Toledo Bend Lake was at a record low, Mr. McDaniel and I organized a "What Went Under" reunion for former residents and/or their descendents of the Robertson Bend community. This community was totally flooded, and everyone lost their homes when the largest man-made body of water in the South was constructed. Between 300-400 people gathered to reminisce about how their homes and property became part of the lake in the early 1960's. Some drove four-wheel vehicles out into the mud to show others where their houses had stood. One house is still intact, although most of the time it is under water. A cemetery was part of the community, and some of the bodies had been reburied at the Macedonia Cemetery prior to filling the lake.

While serving as a member of the Sabine Resource Advisory Committee (RAC), I was able to submit several projects that assisted us with our cemetery research and restoration in Sabine County. RAC develops and recommends projects that benefit national forest land in Shelby and Sabine County. Since a number of old cemeteries are on national forest land or are only accessible via forest service roads, a cemetery project was funded which enabled us to purchase the materials to put up fences, repair fences, and improve the access to historical cemeteries in our county. Another project I submitted allowed us to purchase a sign fabrication machine for the county. This has made it much easier to create or replace road signs, mark trails, and identify cemetery locations in or adjacent to national forest land.

A more personal project involved cleaning up the cemetery in the Black Ankle community. That's where my grandparents, uncles, and aunts are buried. Mr. McDaniel helped me make markers for my grandparents and an uncle's gravesites, and then we held a Marker Dedication Ceremony to honor them. Family members were invited, and both my daughters participated in the event. The markers were made out of cement, and Mr. McDaniel made a plaque for each marker, identifying who was buried there. We attached each plaque to the top of the appropriate marker.

Family members gathered for the Marker Dedication Ceremony.
Lower right next to the cross is one of the cement markers I made.

As Sabine County Historian, Weldon McDaniel is involved with the Milam Settlers Days event held yearly the weekend before Thanksgiving. Milam, Texas, is Sabine County's oldest town and is located about ten miles from Hemphill. Several years after retiring, I was somehow snagged and put on the Milam Settlers Day committee. Together, Mr. McDaniel and I were involved in everything from getting the El Camino Park at Milam set up, to marking the vendor spaces, getting merchants to donate prizes, collecting donations, arranging for fire and police assistance with traffic control, doing trash collection, and cleaning up after the two-day event. I even created a much needed parking lot for the event. The rock was donated by several companies, and I put it down using a county dozer, creating what a contractor would have charged us $15,000 - $20,000 to do. When my daughter planned a family trip to Disneyworld the weekend before Thanksgiving in 2013, I passed my spot on the committee to someone else. Three years is enough time to donate to a specific event; it was time to focus on other community needs.

Another project that I assisted Weldon McDaniel with involved restoring two corn cribs at the Gaines-Oliphint House, located in Pendleton Harbor near Toledo Bend Lake. The house is believed to be the oldest Pre-Republic, Angelo structure existing today in Texas. It was built around 1818, near the ferry on the Sabine River. We actually cut and peeled the poles we used in an attempt to make them look as authentic as possible. The James Frederick Gomer Chapter of Daughters of the Republic of Texas gave us plaques to recognize our contribution to their restoration of this property. Pioneer Day is held the third Saturday in April, and it is a fund raiser for restoration of the house. I have been assisting with keeping up the grounds of the property during the year and for Pioneer Day, in addition to helping with set-up, I collect donations and door prizes.

Because I am always willing to volunteer my time and labor, I get called frequently by individuals and organizations to assist with their projects. I find it very difficult to say no when someone asks for help. For the past two years, I have been involved in the Rosevine Gravel Hill Benefit. Rosevine is a community about 10 miles northwest of Hemphill. Their benefit raises money to help community members in need, and they give some scholarships to graduating seniors in the area. I help assemble their stage, take care of the drinks and ice, and solicit donations from others for this worthy event.

When the Patricia Huffman Smith Columbia Museum was preparing to open adjacent to Hemphill's public library, I volunteered to do some of the dirt work around the museum. This was a time when my skill with a dozer came in very handy. This museum officially opened in February, 2011, and it houses the permanent "NASA Remembering Columbia" exhibit.

I've always had a special fondness for the elderly and those folks (child or adult) in bad situations beyond their control. It really angers me to see either being taken advantage of by others. When I was a child, Miss Bessie Thomas was the oldest person in the Thomas Johnson Community. I'd go by daily to check on her and get her water and wood when needed. She had something wrong with her feet and loved to have me rub them, saying they felt so much better when I did that. I'd do whatever she asked of me, from hanging up her wash to getting her groceries. She died in 1989. I've done lawn work, repaired homes, cut up fallen trees, fixed plumbing problems and anything else I could do for the elderly. Many are reluctant to ask you to assist them because they don't have the money for the materials needed. That's not an issue with me. I'll provide both the labor and the cash needed to get the job done.

I think I've been in the "public transportation" business for years without realizing it. Ever since I had my first vehicle, I've been called upon by individuals in the community to run people everywhere, from a hospital in Lufkin, to the doctor in Jasper, to visit a relative out of town, to get food, etc. These calls come at all hours of the day or night. A relative living in another place might call me late at night to check on their parent, knowing if it's needed, I will step up and transport that person to the hospital or run somewhere to get medication for them. It's a good thing I don't mind driving.

With the arrival of Tashay's children, I started being called "Papa." Since both Fay and I are now retired, we have more time to spend with our grandkids, both at their home and ours. I am already exposing Kobe Myles to our family favorites at the dinner table. Since putting on the Smokey the Bear costume for fire prevention presentations was a regular happening for me while with the Forest Service, I was more than willing to make an appearance at Kobe's Pre-K3 class in Beaumont. I had already put the costume on at the house while he was present, and he had been so tickled by it. However, when I walked into his classroom as Smokey the Bear, he burst into tears. I guess he forgot it was only Papa. Smokey has continued to visit Kobe's classroom each year during Fire Prevention Month. I expect I will be doing the same thing when my granddaughter, Laila Jade, starts school.

*Smokey with Kobe's class — he's the little guy second from the right
(I have my "paw" on his shoulder)*

I am ending this autobiography in 2014, although I look forward to having many more years to devote to assisting those around me. I doubt that I will change much though I keep promising Fay I will slow down and spend more time at home. We have taken several vacations since I retired; those were the first vacations for me, and I really enjoyed them. When I was having the problem with my blood pressure and seeing a doctor, he was questioning me about my lifestyle in an attempt to get to the root of the problem. He told me high blood pressure is often stress-related and asked me what hobbies I had. I told him "none." Obviously finding that hard to believe he started listing a number of things he felt fell into the category of "hobbies." When I assured him I didn't do any of the things he listed, he announced, "That's your problem – no hobbies!" It's true I seem to be working all the time, but I also enjoy most of what I am doing. Thus, I have decided, for me, work IS my hobby.

In this book, I have tried to provide you with some idea of what my life was like as a child and on up to the age of 60. My goal was to give you a "sampling" of incidents and events in my life. To include everything would have been impossible and probably quite boring. In order for you to have other perspectives, Fay and I decided to ask some of our family and friends to write their own Felix "story." They follow this section of the book, and I hope you will enjoy them.

Regrettably, there are more "receivers" than "givers" in this world. It has been my nature to give as much of myself as possible and ask nothing in return, except respect as an individual. In my lifetime, I have developed some amazing friendships with both black and white people. The color of one's skin is not as important to me as the way that person acts toward others. However, I am proud of my heritage and through this autobiography, I hope to pass on some of it to my grandchildren, great grandchildren, and generations that come later. I also desire to see us return to developing a strong work ethic in our children, so they will be productive adults. Too many children give up too early in their lives. All my life I have encountered situations where the "door" was closed and rather than give up, I kept trying other "doors," until I eventually found one that opened for me. I am asking that same thing of my descendents – have the courage and strength to pursue your dreams and NEVER GIVE UP!

Felix Holmes Jr.
April, 2014

While in the process of writing my autobiography, I also began work on a project I wanted to do in memory of my daddy, Felix Holmes. Pictured in the above photo is the barbecue pit I have erected (as of December 2015) on the original site of my parents' old cafe and barbecue pit in the Thomas Johnson Community. Eventually I want to place a historical marker there with information about the cafe. The bricks I used to build the pit came from a building across from the Sabine County Courthouse that was torn down 6-7 years ago (I remember that building from my youth). In addition to the marker, I also intend to install a wood cook stove that is over a 100 years old.

These are two views of the barbecue pit on February 10, 2016.

SECTION THREE:
WHAT OTHERS HAVE TO SAY

This section contains a collection of written pieces about me from friends and relatives. When Fay and I started working on my life story, we decided to ask some of the folks closest to us to share their insights and/or memories about me. We thought you might enjoy reading the "Felix" stories others had to tell. I am indebted to each individual that shared their recollections and feelings with me.

Doing a controlled burn

Felix (Bubba) Holmes
My Husband, Soul Mate, Better Half, and Best Friend
by Gloria "Fay" Holmes

When Bubba and I started working on his autobiography, I knew I would want to tell my "version" of some of his memories. I've known Bubba since my early childhood. We met the summer of 1964 when I was visiting my mother in Hemphill, Texas. At the time, she was married to his cousin, Joe Dupree, who lived next door to Bubba. I could only visit in the summer because, during the school year, I lived in San Augustine, Texas, with my grandmother who was raising me. I was eight years old and he was ten the summer we met, and it was love at first sight when I saw his pretty curly hair. After getting to know him, I asked my mom and Joe to bring him with them anytime they came to visit my grandmother. Most weekends that they visited, Bubba would come with them. I had so much fun when they took us on our first kiddie date to a fair in Center, Texas. As long as we were walking around, eating, and playing carnival games, Bubba was good with that. However, when I asked him to get on some rides with me, he refused. Joe repeatedly encouraged him to try a ride; finally, he reluctantly agreed to get on one. Bad idea! As soon as the ride started going fast, Bubba began crying and screamed to get off; the operator literally stopped the ride to remove him. Although I was disappointed, he had me laughing at the stunt he pulled. From that time on, a bond existed between us, and I would look forward to seeing him at my mom's house in Hemphill or with my mom and Joe when they came to see my grandmother.

When my mom and stepdad divorced after seven years of marriage, I lost all contact with Bubba. My heart was really saddened because our friendship was very special to me. Ten years after our initial meeting in 1964, I was at a carnival in San Augustine, and to my amazement, I spotted him at a distance talking to his cousin. Wanting to be sure it was him before I said anything, I circled back and he was still standing in the same spot visiting with his cousin. I said, "Aren't you Bubba?" to which he replied, "Yes, and you are Louise's daughter." I experienced the same feeling I had when I met him for the first time years ago. We talked for a short while before I told him I had to leave because it was a school night. After I got back to my mom's apartment in San Augustine (I was visiting her), I saw him drive by, but I didn't go outside to meet him.

A week later at school, I saw Bubba's cousin, Betty Jenkins. I told her about running into him at the carnival and asked her to give Bubba my telephone number for my grandmother's house. Instead of calling, undoubtedly because he was interested in getting together again, he got directions from her and drove to San Augustine the next Sunday afternoon. It was September 1974, and my cousin and I were strolling down Farm Road 147 when he passed by looking for my house. Turning around, he followed me home. We sat in his car and talked and before he left, he asked if he could come back the next weekend. I was overjoyed to say, "Yes!"

A friendship that began when I was eight and he was ten developed into a serious relationship within four months. I was drawn to him because he was respectful, compassionate, considerate, and very kind to my family. We were deeply in love, and Bubba asked me to marry him. When I told him I would have to think about it, he said if I agreed to marry him, he would promise to be a good husband to me and a good father to my son. He knew the secret to winning my heart – accepting my son and treating him with kindness and showing respect to my grandmother. I was still hesitant about marriage at that time because my grandmother had recently been in the hospital, and it was my responsibility to give her a daily insulin shot. I couldn't see myself leaving her when she needed me the most. Bubba eased my mind when he promised to take me to San Augustine each morning before he went to work to give her the shot. Being that he had captured my heart again, I couldn't take a chance on losing contact a second time, so I agreed to marry him on December 20, 1974. He did keep his promise concerning the shot, and we drove to San Augustine for several weeks after our marriage before I was able to teach my cousin, who also lived with my grandmother, to give her the shot.

Young and excited about getting married, we only had $25 to make it official. Since we didn't have any extra money, Bubba was unable to buy me a ring or take me on a honeymoon. He sprayed the car windows with white shoe polish to announce "Just Married" and tied a string of cans under his car to draw attention to us. Then he drove around the Hemphill School and through the East Mayfield community in his clean, gold, Fairlane Ford to show off the fact that we were married. Happy to be together, we headed to his mom's house to get her approval of the marriage. She obviously wasn't very happy about sharing her baby and only son with another woman and demanded proof of our marriage.

Bubba had been taking care of his mother for years and had no money saved to get his own place. He knew we would have to live with her for a while, but he assured me that he was going to work hard to get us our own home. He worked at the Forest Service during the day and evening and weekends, he did odd jobs to get extra money. Being a newlywed, I was lonely when he wasn't around, and I developed a lot of anxiety knowing his mom didn't really want us there. To calm my nerves, I began smoking. Bubba made it very clear to me that he wouldn't tolerate smoking saying, "I despise a woman who smokes because when I was very young I had to walk to Beanville, both before and after school, to get cigarettes for my mom." For almost two years I continued to use cigarettes even after he had informed me that if I wanted to smoke, we would not be able to stay together. To save our marriage, I finally stopped. I will always be grateful to him for demanding I quit a habit which could have led to future health problems.

Bubba began to teach our first two children good work ethics early in their lives. As you have read in his autobiography, he started out having to work at a very young age in order to survive. Our kids had specific chores as soon as they were old enough to perform them. Wanting to teach them responsibility, he modeled what that entailed and definitely instilled it in them. His family came first with him as he worked hard to provide us with the things we needed as well as some things we desired. Early in our marriage, he didn't want me working; he preferred I stay home with the kids. I didn't work outside the home until Tashay was about two years old, and then it was only on weekends at Frontier Park Restaurant. He took care of the children the weekends I worked. Bubba was the main disciplinarian in our household when the kids were growing up. If they started to misbehave, I would say, "I'm going to tell your daddy when he gets home," and that worked every time. The teachers at school used the same tactic, threatening to call Felix if they didn't correct their behavior. Being typical mischievous children, they received their share of "whippings." Any time Cedric or Tashay would get sick during the night, Bubba would be the one to get out of bed and go to their aid. Cedric frequently had nighttime nose bleeds, and Bubba knew how to get them stopped. Whatever the problem, he would find a solution. The children had lots of love and respect for him.

Tashay was almost ten years old before Felondria was born. Having a new baby brought a lot of joy to our family. Bubba and his aunt were able to get me to Lufkin Memorial Hospital just in time. When I went into labor that Monday morning, Cedric and Tashay had become so excited and felt the arrival of a new sibling was a reason to miss school. Bubba was proud to be a father again. Since I had been working at Brookeland ISD, I needed to return to work after six weeks at home. Bubba, knowing that concerned me, made sure Felondria had one of the best babysitters available, an elderly lady that lived directly across the street from us. I went back to work in peace, knowing I didn't have to worry about my baby getting good care.

I had started taking college classes in 1984, two years before Felondria was born. After she started Pre-K, I enrolled in more classes. Tashay and Bubba took care of her while I attended college classes at night. I was really getting tired of having to leave my family to attend these courses. I finally completed my Associate of Science in Interdisciplinary Studies. Bubba became my cheerleader as well as my inspiration. He told me if I had made it that far, I needed to go on and get my teacher's certificate, so I could get paid for my skills. Although I wanted to give up, his encouragement and moral support helped me complete my degree in elementary education.

Left to right: Cedric, Felix, Felondria, Fay, Tashay

During Felondria's childhood, Bubba was frequently out of town fighting wildfires on forest service land. I had to assume the role of disciplinarian, but I knew I could always count on him to call daily and check on his family. The kids knew to obey because he would always tell them to mind me whether he was home or not. Anytime he was home, he involved himself in school functions. Upon returning from a trip, he always brought us something to show that he had been thinking of us while he was gone. He was truly a great father throughout our children's childhoods and on into adulthood. My girls and I have never had to worry about our cars being serviced, washed, or running low on gas. That was a responsibility he assumed out of respect for us.

Although I am a very friendly person, I'm not very talkative. Anytime we are going to be around a large group of people, I tell Bubba to be the mouthpiece for both of us, since initiating a conversation with people I don't know is not easy for me. Bubba's advice: "If you will listen to the news, you will know what is going on in the world and have something to talk about." His favorite TV station is CNN, anytime of the day or night; he doesn't miss the local news either. His ability to interact with people is phenomenal. If he says he's going to Brookshire's and will be back in about 15 minutes, those minutes always turn into an hour or more. I'm always meeting people who tell me how much they love being in his company. With his unique sense of humor and magnetic personality, he's the friendly comedian that friends, family, and associates look forward to seeing on a daily basis.

Bubba and I strongly believe in showing kindness and compassion to others. We worked to instill the same kind of values in our children and have watched them inspire people they come in contact with. Bubba has worn many hats in our family; he's been a doctor, plumber, carpenter, electrician, auto mechanic, chef, attorney, and the list goes on. Many of the skills he has acquired he learned through first hand observation and the willingness to get in there and assist with the job. His many talents have saved us a great deal of money over the years. He's also been able to use his knowledge to help relatives, friends, the community, and even complete strangers. Being such a friendly and outgoing person, he has touched many lives and developed a legacy that will, hopefully, inspire his future generations.

As I mentioned earlier, Bubba and I were not financially able to afford a real wedding in 1974. Thus, to celebrate our silver wedding anniversary (25 years), we decided to renew our vows on December 18, 1999, at 6:00 p.m. Bubba said, "Since I didn't do it right at first, we are going to have a real wedding this time." I was so excited to actually have a formal wedding with all three of our children part of the wedding party. Along with other relatives, we created memories we still share to this day. We started out young and poor, so this represented a great accomplishment for the two of us.

No marriage is free of storms; the secret is knowing how to weather them and become closer as a result. Both Bubba and I have had to make many compromises to keep peace in the family. I am very grateful that he has been a caring father and husband throughout our years of marriage. Soon we will celebrate our 40th wedding anniversary. It has taken compromise, communication, and most of all "love" to make it through four decades together as husband and wife. We are two different people; therefore, it is quite normal for us to disagree. The key is being able to resolve our differences, which we have done. Knowing he had disappointed or angered me, he often shows up with a gift as a peace offering to get out of the doghouse.

Bubba is known to show acts of kindness spontaneously and frequently. One that I will relate here involved Joe Dupree's mom (Mrs. Geraldine Dupree), who was also Bubba's great aunt. Knowing she was celebrating her 100th birthday on June 17, 2010, Bubba decided to give her a birthday party, complete with a cake, party treats, and barbecue for family/friends to enjoy. She was so happy and said, "I've never had a birthday party...thank you, thank you!" He made arrangements for Megan Strickland from the Sabine County Reporter, our local newspaper, to come to her home and interview her. The article, along with a photo of Mrs. Dupree and Bubba, was printed in the paper. She passed away on July 7, 2011. Bubba was honored to have been able to create a happy memory for her late in her life. It's a fact that Bubba gets great joy from making others happy.

Turning 60 years old has slowed Bubba down just a little. When his fire-fighting position with the Forest Service took him all over the country, he promised me he would take me to some of those places when we both retired. Well, that hasn't happened yet, but I'm not going to let him off the hook. I intend to plan and book trips to get him out of the county away from all the "new" jobs he has acquired. When he is home, we enjoy preparing and canning vegetables together during the summer months. Being an outdoors person, he is also taking an interest in landscaping our yard, and I'm really happy about that. I am looking forward to spending the rest of my life with Bubba, my husband who has a character like a diamond that shines in the darkest places, and a giving heart which he has and always will share with others. He will lend a helping hand to anyone who is in need. One thing I've learned after forty years with Bubba is the fact that he has to be engaged in some type of activity. Even when he's asleep, he is not still. The lights are out, but that mind of his is operating at full speed. When he arises at dawn, he's off to be of service to someone. Bubba is my **HERO!!!**

Special birthday to be celebrated this week by Geraldine Dupree

by Megan Strickland
Sabine County Reporter

The year was 1910, Halley's comet was making a rare appearance visible to the human eye, William H. Taft was president of the United States, and the Sabine County Courthouse was nearing completion. Few can be found to recall these times, and it's not a great surprise, the life expectancy at the time was only 52 years. One who was around to witness this era of yesteryear was Mrs. Geraldine Dupree, of Hemphill, who, on June 17 will celebrate her 100th birthday.

Born in the Black Ankle community of San Augustine, the second of four daughters and six sons of Ross and Annie Jenkins, Mrs. Dupree remembers days when Sabine County had no means of transportation was rugged dirt roads by horse and buggy, and growing cotton or subsistence farming was a way to make a living.

During her years, Mrs. Dupree has spent days alongside her late husband, Joseph, picking cotton, and doing housework, and raising children. Her later

Reporter photo by Megan Strickland

Special birthday...

Mrs. Geraldine Dupree of Hemphill will celebrate her 100th birthday on June 17. She is shown here with her nephew, Felix Holmes.

decades included receiving her beautician's license from Sweaty's Beauty College in Tyler in 1960. In 1993, at 83 years old, Mrs. Dupree was volunteering at Pineland Early Learning Center, showing that you are never too old to chase about youngsters.

Of her many careers, Mrs. Dupree seemed to remember picking cotton most fondly, saying, "We'd get up at dusk, go pick the cotton. Come in at lunch, make lunch for my husband, go pick the cotton. Cook dinner and do chores. Wake up the next day, and start all over."

While Mrs. Dupree doe n't really give preference one decade over the oth she does miss the w: things were in days past.

"This new fashion wo1 last long. That old fashion ain't going nowhere Dupree said.

In the present, M1 Dupree spends her days g(ting around pretty we. according to nephew Fel Holmes and son, Joe L Dupree. Although a cane necessary for her to wal she still does laundry a1 washes dishes.

This is quite a feat sin(according to data availab from 2008, only abo1 90,000 of 350 million pe(ple in the United States li\ to be a centenaria1 Currently a movement 1 document and study cent(narians is underway, hov ever, Mrs. Dupree doesh cite any particular diet (lifestyle to be her reason sb lived 99 years before ev(having to visit the docto instead she says, it was th work of a higher power.

"I do know the Lord ju1 blessed me, deeply so."

SUNRISE	SUNSET
June 17, 1910	July 7, 2011

Daddy
by Tashay Prejean

When my parents asked me to write something for my dad's autobiography, I knew I wanted to briefly touch upon those things in my childhood that quickly come to mind. Chores were important in our home. My brother and I were not yet teenagers when we had a list of chores to complete each week. We could never keep track of our weekly duties, so my dad had us sign a "chore contract." This contract kept us on track because if the chores were not completed, trouble followed. According to my dad, we no longer had any excuse for "forgetting" what had to be done.

Early in life, my dad taught me a strong work ethic. I can remember picking blueberries during the summer to earn a little spending money. Although I could buy whatever I wanted, my dad always cautioned me to "save some for a rainy day."

My dad's "wake-up call" was the signal to get ready for school each morning. He often had to call me one, two, maybe even three times before I would get up. One morning he decided to teach me a lesson. He called me one time and I didn't get up. I was relying on the next call, but it never came. I'll spare you the details of how I missed a test at school, but needless to say, I learned a valuable lesson that day: answer your first call because there may not be another.

I had this little black hat that I often wore when I dressed up. One weekend I got ready to go to the movies (complete with the little black hat) and to my dismay, my dad had other plans for me. I was supposed to have done some chores and other things he had asked me to do during that week; however, I hadn't gotten around to them. Since the chores were still waiting for me, he refused to allow me to go to the movies. I couldn't believe he was telling me I had to stay home after I had spent all that time getting dressed up with my little black hat. He definitely taught me to take care of business first and pleasure later. By the way, my dad still has that little black hat.

I'm a bit of a speed demon, and I love to drive fast. I can remember getting speeding tickets and, with a call to my dad, relying on him to take care of them. Eventually his patience wore out (I'm sure his concern for my safety was also a factor), and he warned me not to get another ticket. When I did get my next ticket, I took care of it on my own, figuring it was best my dad knew nothing about it. To my surprise, he did find out about the ticket; I hadn't realized a receipt would be mailed to my home address. I came to the realization, early in my life, that I couldn't keep anything from my dad. He either always knew or somehow found out about anything I thought I had cleverly concealed from him.

My dad has taught me so many life lessons that have shaped me into the woman I am today. He encouraged me daily to strive to be the best and to never give up. He frequently told me that anything worth having doesn't come easily, and hard work pays off. As an adult, I am inspired by his intelligence, selflessness, and generosity. My dad is my hero, and I appreciate him each and every day for his guidance, leadership, and unconditional love.

I have been blessed with a great dad. Now my own children get to benefit in a similar fashion with the best "papa" grandkids could have. The values my dad instilled in me are now being instilled in my children for which I am truly grateful. Mere words do not begin to describe how fortunate I am to have Felix Holmes as my dad and how blessed Kobe and Laila are to have him as their papa.

Though time and space prevent it, I could easily go on and on about my dad because he really is an unbelievable angel here on earth. He has touched so many lives with his "giving heart," and he continues to do so each and every day.

I love you, Daddy! You are and always will be my HERO!!

Mr. Felix "Bubba" Holmes
by Don Eddings

They say to find a true friend in this life is one of life's greatest gifts, but to have a friendship that will last for over forty years is honestly a treasure from God above. I have been fortunate enough to stumble across this type of friendship with my dear friend, Mr. Felix "Bubba" Holmes. From fighting forest fires in the cruel daunting elements of nature, to fixing a car's alternator in the backyard, Bubba has always been the first to show up with eager helping hands, always ready to help a friend in need.

I suppose my first encounter with Mr. Holmes was when I was just a junior in high school. I was involved in the YCC, and my boss was none other than Felix. We had been assigned the most prestigious of jobs – collecting pulpwood down FM 944 and little did I know that it was that job that would set the course for a lifelong friendship. While Felix was busy cutting the wood, I had the job of measuring it. As the job went on, I decided to have some fun with my new boss and as he cut down the end of our track, Felix made the comment that the sticks had been getting shorter and shorter. I smiled a mischievous grin, mainly to myself, and snickered quietly. He asked, "What's your problem, boy? How come these measurements are getting smaller and smaller from these woods?" I looked up at him and said, "You mean to tell me I wasn't suppose to cut the wood shorter?" With a laugh he shook his head and said, "Well, come on, let's finish up. Since you already screwed up this track, keep cutting them short, maybe they won't notice it too much." Ever since then I suppose you could say we have been inseparable and honestly, I wouldn't have it any other way.

In 1979, I found employment with the U.S. Forest Service and lo and behold, Bubba and I were put together once again. It was with him that I would find my traveling partner, of sorts, on wildfires. From California to North Carolina, Bubba and I traveled all across the country, putting out fires and bickering and arguing like brothers all the way. On several different occasions, many people thought that our banter would lead to us fighting in public. However, our supervisor would just laugh and say, "Just leave them alone. They do this constantly." Even with all the bickering, I soon came to realize that I couldn't have asked for a better traveling buddy. When we were actually on a fire line in who-knows-where, it was reassuring to know that even out there in the dead of night, on the cold hard ground, my family thousands of miles away, I was never really truly alone. My best friend was right there in the tent next to me. Although it wasn't like being at home in my recliner, it made things a little more tolerable.

I could go on and tell about all our stories, but I think I would run out of paper before I ran out of our adventures together. He has been my traveling buddy, my partner in work, my personal BBQ chef and above all, my truest friend in life. In this time in our society, trusting someone completely with not only your life but the lives of your family, is almost an impossible feat for anyone to achieve...except for me. I am lucky enough to say that I can. Bubba Holmes is a man of honesty, loyalty, integrity, and truly the best friend anyone could ever ask for. These traits are also reflected in his lovely wife and beautiful family. I know that wherever I am, near or far, I can trust him and his family to take care of mine and do for them when I cannot. Likewise, he can rest assured I will return the favor for him and his family. No matter what decision Mr. Holmes makes, I am a hundred percent sure I will agree with him. I always have, and I always will.

<u>Note from Felix:</u>
Don is the brother I never had. A very special bond exists between us. No matter how much we argue or disagree, we remain the best of friends. It is only with your best friend that you can let down all your defenses, knowing he will stick with you through thick and thin.

Felix Holmes, Jr.
by Ernest Weldon McDaniel

Why am I up at four in the morning writing down my thoughts about Felix Holmes, Jr.? He will be referred to in this narrative as either Felix or Bubba. Let me introduce myself. I am Ernest Weldon McDaniel, a native and resident of Sabine County, Texas, fourteen years older than Felix, white Anglo, retired teacher and school administrator, Sabine County Historian, genealogist, cemetery preservationist, husband, father, grandfather, great-grandfather, and a friend of Felix. In fact one could say with certainty that he is my best friend. My above mentioned qualifications probably give me the right to tell some very serious and sometimes humorous stories and encounters with the above mentioned subject, Felix Holmes, Jr.

These thoughts about Felix are being recorded at the request of his lovely and gracious wife of many years, Gloria Mosley Holmes. She is the one who has the most to say about him, hopefully all positive.

Any statements or words said about the subject are not meant to be derogatory, demeaning, disparaging or to cast any negative thoughts about the same. We have known each other a very long time and say things to one another that any bystander might interpret in the wrong way.

It is now time to stop the "I" and "me" part of this story and try to record some of the thoughts and experiences this author has had while knowing Felix since the early nineteen seventies.

Ancestry

Felix's paternal grandfather was Handy Holmes, who is listed in the 1880 US Population Census as Mulatto, twenty-two years old, born in Texas, and wife, Ella Thomas Holmes, also listed as Mulatto, twenty years old, born in Texas. According to Sabine County, Texas marriage records, they married on 1 Jan 1880. In the 1900 census, he is listed as forty years old with wife Ella and eight children. The youngest child listed is Able (Felix, Sr.) at four years old. All ten members of the household are listed as Black. The Mulatto designation in the 1880 census usually indicates one Black parent and one White Anglo parent.

As listed in the Sabine County, Texas Death Records, Handy Holmes died on 14 Aug 1942. Since there is no birth record and using census records, Handy was between 82 and 84 years of age when he died. Ella's death certificate lists her death date as 6 Jun 1946. Since her age is given in the 1880 census as twenty and the 1900 census as 36 and the 1910 census as forty-five, she was probably between eight-one and eighty-six years old at her death.

Felix Holmes, Sr. according to his tombstone was born 13 Oct 1895 and died 30 Nov 1960. He enlisted in the US Army on 22 Aug 1918 and served as a private in the 11th Co. 165th Depot Brigade, serving until 16 Dec 1918. He was assigned to Camp Travis near Tyler, Texas. His discharge papers are on file in the Sabine County Courthouse. Felix, Sr. married Louella Dupree. She was born 21 Jul 1917 and died 10 Jul 1993. Louella Dupree Holmes, Felix, Jr.'s mother, was the daughter of Angelo Dupree and Elizabeth Coutee. Angelo was born to Noah and Mary E. Dupree on 2 Oct 1886 in Louisiana and died 15 Feb 1969 in San Augustine County, Texas. Elizabeth was the daughter of Seraphim and Luvinia Coutee.

Both Angelo and Elizabeth Coutee Dupree were born on the Cane River south of Natchitoches, Louisiana, which brings in a complicated mixture of races. This fact makes Felix, Jr. a bi-racial mix of probably French, Black African, White Anglo, and Indian. The French Acadians were exiled from Canada to several locations, one being South Louisiana where they mixed with Black, White Anglo, and remnant Indian populations and developed into what is sometimes referred to as Creoles or Acadians. In the early US Census, these residents are listed as Mulatto. As a child, because of his bi-racial ancestry, he was continually taunted seriously and sometimes for fun about his race. Normally this would have made a typical youth possibly bitter or at least develop a resentful attitude toward adults, but he didn't.

The Early Years

Since this author only became acquainted with Felix in the nineteen seventies, very little is known about his early years other than he grew up in deep poverty. His father died when he was six years old. Soon after his father's death, Felix was trying to help his mother survive, being left without any income. By the time he was six, he was dragging old refrigerator and stove boxes two miles from the stores in Hemphill for the purpose of insulating the house from the cold. During this time period, the USDA was donating commodities (food stuff) to needy families. Commodities were passed out in Hemphill and had to be dragged home in a toe sack (burlap) bag.

Felix survived one setback after the other. Time spent in school was probably limited, but he overcame. One would surmise that he would grow into his teenage years with a very poor attitude toward society, but he didn't.

High School and the YCC Years

In his high school years, at 15 years old (1969), Felix started working during the summer in the YCC Program conducted by the US Forest Service. This program took disadvantage youth and placed them in a work program in order to learn job skills related to the forest industry and some life skills. The program must have worked on Felix. After high school, on 10 Dec 1973, he took a permanent job with the US Forest Service which he kept until his retirement on 4 August 2007. This author came into contact with Felix at about the end of his YCC days.

The author's father, Nolan Ernest McDaniel, Jr. (NEM), had started working for the Forest Service in the mid-1940's and was still there when Felix started working. NEM had a hard upbringing, similar to Felix, and had always had a soft spot in his heart for the underdog. Being the first black man to start working with a group of all white male workers was tough. NEM and several others provided some protection to Felix from sometimes unkind and prejudicial individuals. Felix had recently married and was trying to begin a family which was hard in rural East Texas.

The author had already left home to seek his fortune in 1957 and lived away from Sabine County from 1961-1976. On trips home, Felix was occasionally at NEM's house to pick up some item or garden produce. This is where we met. In 1967, the author moved back to the county and finished a career in public education, retiring in 1998. After retiring, the author started promoting tourism and the history of Sabine County full time on a volunteer basis.

When Felix retired in 2007, he started helping the author who was already providing volunteer services dealing with cemetery preservation, history presentations in East Texas and Western Louisiana, and family history searches (genealogy) for individuals, the annual Pioneer Day, Milam Settlers Day, and historical marker dedications. While working with the committees in certain organizations, Felix saw some prejudice toward blacks. One would have thought this would have soured his attitude toward volunteer work, but it didn't.

The Scrounge

By dictionary definition, a scrounge is defined as: to get by begging or sponging, mooching or to pilfer. While securing donations and items for our volunteer work, we have never stolen or done anything unethical, although we have come close several times. Because Felix grew up using every known resource to survive, he became a master at securing needed items for meetings, festivals, marker dedications, and other events sponsored by the Sabine County

Historical Commission, Milam Settlers Day, Pioneer Day, and other volunteer organizations in Sabine County. He is a second term member of the Sabine County Historical Commission. Felix's attitude is that it doesn't hurt to ask.

Usually Bubba is very successful in securing needed items without charge and often more than is needed for a specific event, so the extra is held over till the next event. While scrounging, nearly begging, almost sponging, close to mooching, he does sometimes take a verbal abusing that might make most have less than desirable thoughts about the perpetrator, but he doesn't.

On Time

Since volunteering with Felix since 2007, we have spent hundreds of days mending cemetery fences, mowing festival grounds, mowing, cleaning and fencing old forgotten cemeteries, repairing the roof on some old historic building, compiling a burial index for an old cemetery, and many other volunteer tasks, too many to mention.

Out of the hundreds of times he was suppose to meet the author at some location to perform one of the tasks mentioned earlier, the occasions he has arrived on time could be counted on one hand. The only good thing about Felix showing up late is that he always arrives with a load of needed materials or items he acquired by stopping and talking to someone. One would think, because of waiting sometimes up to three hours for Felix to arrive, that this author would have developed a bad attitude toward Felix, but he hasn't.

Note from Felix:
Mr. McDaniel is my mentor, as well as a special friend. I have a great deal of respect for him. His counsel and great wisdom has enriched my life beyond measure.

Felix Holmes
by Nancy Stone

I became acquainted with Felix Holmes through his wife, Gloria, when I started teaching with her in August 2005. Though initially I only knew him as a hard-working man who obviously cared deeply for his family, I eventually came to realize he was one of the most unique individuals I had ever encountered in my life. As Gloria and I became close friends, I had more opportunities to either visit with Felix and/or observe him in action. I quickly discovered he gives new meaning to the expression "lend a helping hand." Relatively new to Hemphill (my husband and I bought our home in 2000), we started commenting on the fact that we seemed to run into Felix everywhere we went in the county and most of the time, he was helping someone – everything from picking up groceries for a neighbor to repairing a roof for an elderly lady to driving someone to the doctor in Pineland, etc., etc. – I think you get the message. If you had the chance to chat with the individual he was helping, you often discovered he was giving more than his time – he was also buying the groceries, providing the roofing materials, and paying the doctor's bill. It became apparent to us that Felix has a big heart for those in need.

In addition to continually encountering Felix in the community, we also began to realize that he was a wealth of information about Hemphill and the surrounding area. We began to rely on him when we needed to know where to go to obtain a specific part for a broken item or who provided a service we required. He was our version of "Angie's List." Everyone you talked to seemed to know Felix, and many had more than one story to relate about how he had helped them. I discovered early on in our friendship that Felix never made "idle" promises. If he told you he was going to do something, it definitely happened regardless of the many other commitments he might have or the way he felt (health-wise) on a particular day.

I was delighted when I heard Felix and Gloria were going to write his autobiography because I thought it might help to explain how he became the person he is today - a man who may not quote scripture yet daily puts into practice the teachings in the Bible. I seriously doubt, knowing how humble both Felix and Gloria are, that they will even begin to touch upon the many ways he has helped others and/or the contributions he has made to his community. Part of what makes Felix truly unique is his philosophy toward life. In some lengthy conversations with him, I was amazed at his upbeat attitude and what he has been able to take away from incidents over the years that have involved him. He's an embodiment of the expression, "When life gives you lemons, make lemonade." I wish there was a way to bottle and redistribute what it is that constitutes the man Felix "Bubba" Holmes. If we could do that, we would create a much better world!

Mrs. Nancy Stone

Felix Holmes and Marc Harris
by Barb Harris

In February of 1992, Marc and I transferred to the Sabine National Forest. Marc became the Recreation and Fire Officer for the Yellowpine District.

Not too long after Marc started working there, he would come home talking about this employee named Felix who had a great disposition, was a hard worker, and was a great barbeque cook. What worried Marc was that the staff was taking advantage of Felix. Felix would do anything for anyone, from barbequing a pig all night, to mowing someone's lawn and still coming into work on time, to do his job. He was expected to do these things outside his position without as much as a thank you. Felix did whatever was asked with a smile on his face but a bit of pain in his eyes. Marc was not Felix's supervisor and could not stop this abuse.

Somewhere along the line, I am not sure how, but Marc managed to become Felix's supervisor, and the world changed for both of them. Felix began calling Marc "Dad," and Marc called Felix "Son," and in some loving way, they both relished their new relationship.

Marc Harris

I can't think of any specific stories except the big one. In March of 1995, Marc had his heart attacks, three of them, eight hours apart. It happened on a Saturday and the doctor told me to get his family here as soon as possible because he was not sure Marc would last very long. I don't remember calling anyone except our families but somehow the word spread, and Felix was one of the first at the hospital.

I have never seen anyone who looked as stricken as Felix. From Saturday evening until the following Thursday, Felix was there. I know he came and went, but he always seemed to be there to support Marc and encourage him to fight and get well. It is something I will never forget, such love.

I don't seem able to remember all the stories that Marc told; however, someone should ask Felix about the new engine the Yellowpine District got and his "ownership" of it. As I recall, Don got into some trouble with Felix about the condition of the engine after Don's use. Also, I recall Felix went hunting for a large hog and got into some sort of trouble with capturing the hog. Also, Felix should be able to describe the many times he helped with all the prescribed burning and tell some of the stories.

I do know that if I ever needed help no one would come faster than Felix. He may not be of my blood, but he sure as heck is my family and certainly was Marc's.

Note from Felix:

Marc Harris was a forester in charge of Recreation and Fire for the Yellowpine District. He and his wife had moved here from Oklahoma. Marc and I developed a relationship based on trust and respect. When he became my supervisor, he told me he knew I always had his back — he saw the way I worked and respected me for my knowledge. I became very close to Marc and his wife, and when he retired and moved back to Oklahoma City, I made sure I visited him there a couple of times before his death.

Felix Holmes
by Joe Bell

Being raised in the same neighborhood, I have known Felix all his life. I knew his parents and siblings, though most of our personal interactions have been as adults. As an older adolescent, one does not have daily interaction with those that are several years younger. However, being from a small community, I was very aware of Felix's presence. When I left home for college, Felix was probably in middle school.

As a young man, I would see Felix on my infrequent visits back to Hemphill. By this time he had graduated from high school and was a young adult. He and my father, Willie Bell, had established a relationship that would last throughout my father's life. On one of these visits, I learned that Felix had married and begun a family. This was a surprise to me because, as I recall, Felix was somewhat of a connoisseur of fine distilled spirits! On subsequent visits, I recall seeing Felix and his growing family.

It was gratifying to see that Felix had turned his life around and become a major contributor to his community and a strong family man. As I alluded to earlier, his initial path was not a predictor of his current success. From my perspective, he is a self-made man who could have easily chosen a different path.

Fortunately for me, Felix and his family became very close to my parents. Being thousands of miles away from my parents, it was comforting to know they had someone dependable close by. Recently, upon reviewing my family photos, I saw several pictures of the Holmes family interacting with my parents. Because Felix is a "jack-of-all-trades," he was of immeasurable value to my father. Additionally he was someone upon whom my father could bestow his "words of wisdom."

Joe Bell, son of Willie Bell, with Fay and Felix

Felix was the primary reason that my father was included in the information on blacks in the early history of East Texas. He worked tirelessly gathering information and artifacts that belonged to my father. His effort toward this project shows that he is a determined, resourceful, and dedicated man. I am very pleased that Felix cared enough for my father to take on this momentous task. He obviously cared for him.

I am very appreciative that Felix was in my father's life. I know the relationship was mutually beneficial; though Felix may not have thought so when a certain mule was involved! Personally, I am proud to call Felix my friend and always look forward to visiting him and his family each time I am in Hemphill.

Willie "Sweetie" Bell

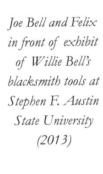

Joe Bell and Felix in front of exhibit of Willie Bell's blacksmith tools at Stephen F. Austin State University (2013)

A Fine Man
by Suellen Abbott

When you have known someone for most of your life, you know you have a friend. I have known Felix Holmes since he was a young boy and after he grew up, he became a good friend to me and my family. Yes, Felix and his sweet wife are the type of people on whom you can depend. They are kind and nice, cordial and respected people of the community and are certainly friends of mine. I knew Felix and his family when I was young, especially his mother. She was a sweet and kind lady who believed in hard work and living a good life filled with the highest of true values. Therefore, she instilled these qualities in her son, Felix. He and his family lived in the Thomas Johnson Community, just outside the city limits of Hemphill. I knew the community well, as I was one of the first white teachers to go to the colored school which was called Thomas Johnson. Of course, this was in another time and era many years ago, before segregation. I had the privilege of teaching Felix, as I taught music in grades one through eight. We learned a lot, had many good times, and presented many great musical programs for everyone's enjoyment in the community. After several years when segregation was implemented in the state of Texas, all students attended Hemphill School where Felix finished his education. The traits that were instilled in him at home, as well as at school, helped mold him into the great man he is today! He is a person who always extends a helping hand, as well as always respects others. He certainly is friendly and wants only the best for his family, his community, and friends. He certainly is admired for all of his outstanding qualities that he displays every day!

Most of his life's work or employment was a service to Sabine County. He was a revered forester who helped manage the beautiful forest of East Texas. He worked in that field of service for many years until his retirement in 2007. You would think he would just stay at home and enjoy his retirement, but no, he had a new endeavor of service awaiting him. He would blaze a new path as he and Mr. Weldon McDaniel, a former educator, began to diligently work to preserve the history of Sabine County. What a challenge to gather the documentation of pioneer families and all cemeteries located in Sabine County and provide informational archives and facts of long ago, even with photographs! Many cemeteries have had the honor of being placed on the Historical Register of the state of Texas. Beautiful markers have been placed at each old historical site. How thankful we are that these great men have met the task of becoming the "care-takers" of invaluable information that will be preserved for future generations. They have also secured and built the beautiful Sabine County History Center where all of the historical records are placed. It takes a man like Felix to meet an arduous challenge and to help to conquer it because it is for the welfare of mankind. How thankful we should be for his dedicated service and love for the place where he lives.

That's why I can say with assuredness that Felix is truly a kind and respected friend. In recognizing all of his service and achievements to our community, to the town of Hemphill, and to Sabine County, he is certainly known as "A Fine Man" by all who know him. He has contributed so much to the welfare of others. He meets everyone with a big smile and a firm handshake. He is trustworthy, honorable, dependable, and exhibits a true and kind spirit.

I have always treasured knowing Felix and his beautiful wife, Gloria, and their children. I have taught many generations of children and have had the opportunity to know them as adults. When one becomes a fine, respectful, and talented person like Felix, as his teacher, it fills my heart with much pride...what a wonderful reward! Gloria is also a treasured friend. She is also an educator and has taught for many years. She is now retired but has also contributed so much to the children of Sabine County. She is commended for being such a positive role model and inspiration for her students. I have always regarded Gloria and Felix as treasured friends.

We should, with much pride, recognize the dedicated service of Felix Holmes. He has certainly been an asset to Sabine County, to the town of Hemphill, and to his family and friends. We "thank" him for the important work that he has done and for all the long hours of work that have been accomplished. We, as fellow citizens, are so thankful for people like Felix who truly care and love their community and the many people within. We are proud that the past will be preserved for future generations to enjoy and remember. We admire his intuition, his fortitude, and his unselfish loyalty to the welfare of others. I'm glad that I have a "fine man" for a true friend!

Mrs. Suellen Abbott

Felix Holmes Jr.
by Lonnie B. Davis

I have known Felix (or as he is more commonly known: Bubba) all of his life. We both grew up in the Thomas Johnson community. Felix's parents owned a business in the community that was frequented by the community, myself included. Also, I rode Felix's father's school bus to school.

Felix is the embodiment of the adage that a boy becomes a man when a man is needed. Felix's father died when he was a young child. He stepped up and became the man of the house for his mother and youngest sister. He did odd jobs at the school after hours and progressed to other jobs from there. However, Felix did not have to face such a daunting task alone because back then, we had the proverbial village that it is said is required to raise a child. We had the Thomas Johnson School, its principal, teachers and staff, who, in addition to providing an exemplary education, also served as surrogate parents and mentors. Likewise, in the community, everybody's child was everybody else's child. They would feed you if you were hungry. You could accompany their kids on trips. You could watch their television if you did not have one. And, they would dispense the curative medicine that a kid needed for conduct unbecoming.

Felix and I did not interact significantly when we were growing up because he was still in elementary school when I graduated from high school. Then, higher education followed by work took me away from Hemphill until about 1980.

Upon my return to Hemphill, little Felix had become a grown man, was employed by the United States Forest Service, had married his lovely and talented wife Gloria, had built a home, and was raising a family. As though that was not sufficient, Felix knew the identity of and had a relationship with seemingly everybody in Sabine County as well as nearby counties. Make a trip with Felix in East Texas and be prepared to be stopped in every parking lot and store you enter by other patrons wanting to talk to him. Those relationships serve Felix well. Merchants open their stores after hours and even on Sundays for Felix to get a part or a tool, usually to fix something for someone else. Felix has a boundless work ethic. That's why we call him the "Energizer Bunny" (behind his back, of course).

Felix's boundless work ethic served him well. He worked night and day to support his family and to fix everything that broke in the community. He put his wife and kids through college and his oldest daughter, Tashay, through pharmacy school.

In retrospect, it's easy to see why Felix has been successful and earned the respect and admiration of those who know him. Like Cesar's wife, Felix's character and reputation are above reproach. He has the manners of a choir boy. And, he could charm a starving man out of his last morsel of food.

Felix's is a life worthy of emulation by all who would succeed.

Felix and Lonnie Davis

Recollections of Felix
by Greg Cohrs

It's not often that we get the opportunity to let the people that we love know how we feel about them. We should probably do that more, rather than waiting to eulogize. Here are a few recollections of my dear friend and brother, Felix Holmes.

Though we came from different backgrounds, Felix and I are kindred spirits. He is among my very few best friends. To this day, and I suspect to the end of his time on this earth, he remains concerned for my family. Felix and I worked together for more than 21 years. We quickly became more than just work friends, we became more like family. We, and our families, were concerned about each other. We were together through thick and thin, including family celebrations and losses.

I've moved away now, but Felix would rush to my aid if I called him in need right now. During our time together, Felix was always there when he was needed by me or Sandra. In fact, he came to the aid of most anyone in need, often dropping what he had going in order to be able to help others. Oftentimes, he'd help Sandra when I was away on a fire detail or trip. I laugh when I think of the time that Felix rescued Sandra from a possum that had found its way into our trash can during the summer and expired. She wasn't sure it was dead, but it smelled bad. Felix came to her rescue as he always did. We lived in a Forest Service house, so whenever there were problems Felix usually came to the rescue to restore order. On many occasions, he dealt with sewer, water, gas, and frozen pipe issues. He was always willing to help watch over our place and feed the animals when we made trips. He even helped Sandra start the mower a number of times when I was gone.

We had to move to another house in Hemphill after living in the Forest Service house for nearly 14 years. The move was a large undertaking, including the moving of a greenhouse and workshop. Working together in an innovative way using Felix's trailer, we were able to move those large items and lots of other stuff. Many others were involved in the move, but Felix was there most every step of the way. I will never forget when the greenhouse slipped off the trailer and skidded down Highway 184 in front of Rice Street. Felix and I scurried quickly to reload what was left of the greenhouse and clear the road. It's pretty funny now but was just a little stressful at the time. When we got settled into the place on Tanglewood, Felix brought his tractor and bush hog over to help us begin to claim part of the property from the wild into a yard. That was some pretty rough work, but he was right there to help us. He loaned me his DR Trimmer to help clear part of the property. Felix is a skilled sawyer. On many occasions, he cut hazardous trees and branches to help us. I remember one time, in particular, when I was recovering from surgery and he came over and cleaned up our backyard after a thunderstorm broke about a third of the top from a large oak.

At work Felix was the ONE that you chose to take care of the tough jobs or things that needed great care or sensitivity. You could trust that what you asked him to do would be done when you needed it to be done; otherwise, he'd let you know that it couldn't be done that way and alternative arrangements would be necessary. I was a primary Incident Commander related to wildfire and Burn Boss related to prescribed burning. He was my go-to person for so much related to fire, repairs, etc.

I'll always laugh as I remember that Felix and Don Eddings were like an inseparable old married couple. Their constant banter was humorous. I fondly remember the time in 1996 when Felix, Don, and I took the engine down to the Lower Rio Grand National Wildlife Refuge on a fire detail. Once we arrived, they briefed us and told us there was a bounty on any federal officer killed in the area of drug activity. That got our attention, and we were not happy to say the least. However, it turned out to be a good detail, and we had a great time working together. We made patrols along the 150-mile border from Boca Chica Beach to Falcon Lake Dam. The picture below is of our Type 6 Engine on the beach.

Greg Cohrs, Felix, and Don Eddings

On one patrol, we encountered what appeared to be a drug deal going down, so we quickly did a U-turn and left the area. Another time, we found a neat old abandoned farm house, so we stopped to look the place over. Felix was behind me as I approached the door. I began to push the door open when we heard a noise from inside that sounded like someone stepping away from the door. I turned around to see where Felix was, and he'd already fled to and was sitting inside the engine. We decided it best to move along, but we all had a big laugh about that later.

Felix worked for District Ranger Ike Hawkins for a long time. Ike was an old Marine drill instructor. Ike would ask Felix something, and Felix generally responded, "Ranger, let me tell you the truth…" Ike would always cut him off there and ask Felix if that meant he lied to him sometimes. That would fluster Felix; Ike took pleasure in doing that.

I recollect Felix working about 1250 hours on the Texas Blowdown of 1998. That's approaching nearly two years worked in a one-year period! Felix never complained, he just kept plugging away. I could depend on him for whatever critical need I had. It was hard to believe that about 1200 of us worked something like 440,000 hours on that project from February 10th through Thanksgiving out of the Dreka Workcenter.

I suspect that Felix used up two of his nine lives (that's kind of humorous now that I've said that because I often called him "Felix the Cat") on the Temple Fire near Bronson when the fire made crown runs along the flank that Felix and Millard Smith were working. The trees were about 35 feet tall, and the fire would change from a five-foot high ground fire to a fire 50 feet above the crowns when the wind gusted. It was all Felix and Millar could do to outrun the wall of fire two times when it made crown runs toward them. After the second time, we backed off to roads to catch the fire. It was certainly unusual fire activity that terrified and educated us.

Felix was a dependable, hard worker with a great work ethic. He never complained about work. I recollect hearing stories from him regarding some challenging times he had growing up and getting started in the working world. Mr. Gandy had taken Felix under his wing, gave him opportunity, and taught him the right way in terms of work ethic. Felix took that to heart and helped mentor others at every opportunity, even sometimes after they had rejected the help in some way.

Felix is a very devoted husband and father who adores his wife and kids. He wanted them to have the opportunities that he did not enjoy. It was good to be able to celebrate Gloria and Felix's marriage vow renewal, as well as Tashay's Doctor of Pharmacology graduation celebration. It was also good to be able to help (and be trusted with helping) his kids with school work. Sandra and I laughed when Felix always referred to Gloria as "my wife." I'd always ask him who "my wife" was.

Sandra and I, and probably most anyone else who knows Felix well, have fond memories of his hooting laughter when he thinks something is really funny. He always enjoyed a good practical joke, but sometimes things turned and he ended up being the recipient. Regardless, he was always good-natured about it. One story, in particular, that he laughs about and retells involves a bale of cleaning rags delivered to the work center. This particular bale contained ladies underwear for some reason, and much lively practical joking occurred as a result. I'll also never forget his laughter when he told and retold the story of one employee who found a perfectly good piece of carpet rolled up and tossed into a dump. The only problem was that it had a dead animal in it. Once he asked Sandra if she heard him drive by and rap his truck pipes at 5:00 a.m. He just hooted when she told him that she'd "rap those pipes around his head."

Felix is a master cook. Everyone always wanted him to cook for various events and gatherings. His specialties of barbeque brisket, ribs, chicken, and fried fish were favorites. To this day, I've never found barbeque better than Felix's, and I've eaten a lot in many places. I recollect my dad really enjoying his brisket and fish immensely. Dad would always ask about Felix, and Felix always asked how our parents were doing.

I'll always be thankful that God placed Felix and his family in the life of my family. They've truly been a blessing to us in more ways than we can count. The world would be a better place if there were more people like Felix.

Note from Felix:

Greg is a close friend who always encouraged me in my endeavors. I'll never forget the support he gave me when my sister and mom died. Greg is a "word master;" it was the mini-biography he wrote about me for Black History Month a number of years ago that we used to initially "jump-start" my memories for this book. Regrettably, we had to omit a few of the recollections in this piece of writing due to space limitations. However, I am including the entire piece in one of the family history albums I am creating, just as I have kept the little log cabin he made for Tashay and then Felondria to use for school projects.

Felix Holmes and the Pole-Barn
by George E. Avery

I haven't known Felix as long as the other people who have written in this book, but I do have one particular experience with him that indicates he has a profound interest in historical preservation. I first met Felix as part of his activity with Weldon McDaniel—the Sabine County Historian. Felix was his assistant. We did an Oral Interview Project of Sabine, San Augustine, and Nacogdoches Counties, and Weldon and Felix agreed to be interviewed in 2010. I knew the first time I met Felix that he would be called "Creole" in Louisiana today—his ancestors were from Louisiana. This term is not generally used in Texas, but Felix comes from a Creole settlement called Black Ankle, that is north of highway 21 on the San Augustine-Sabine County line. Felix came over for the Creole Heritage Festival in Natchitoches, Louisiana, in 2015. I gave a presentation about "Creoles from Texas" and introduced Felix to the people who came. I think Felix was happy to meet people who might know about his ancestors.

In the winter of 2016, I went to Sabine County to get pictures of Felix's BBQ pit and was talking about a current problem I had with moving an old barn to the Chireno Historical Society property, in eastern Nacogdoches County. I had been trying for about a year to get this barn moved and was not having much luck with it. I mentioned this to Felix, and he said he would see what he could do. Felix contacted a man in Newton County who was interested, but ultimately unable to do it because of the amount of rainfall in the area. Another person, in Louisiana, did not work out, so Felix finally contacted John McKenzie of Lufkin. Mr. McKenzie would need some money to pay for his expenses of helpers and gas, but he would accept whatever we would give him. After securing some money from the Chireno Historical Society, and adding a bit of my own, we finally got the barn moved to Chireno in the early summer of 2016.

This barn complements the Stagecoach Inn and the Baptist Church building on the property. I should have mentioned that we got half of the barn. The other half was connected by the roof, but it housed animals and was more rotten than the half that we got. It would have been good to get the whole barn, but there were too many poles that would have to be replaced, and the roof had caved in. The barn—a pole-barn or crib-barn, was built between 1900, and 1930. We know this based on family information and the fact that wire nails, utilized after 1900 were in the structure. Mike Serres, the husband of the owner, Rebecca Serres, immediately warmed up to Felix who made sure Mike was okay with all the arrangements. Weldon McDaniel, with Felix Holmes' assistance, is taking the lead on building two lean-to attachments to our barn. The design for the lean-to structure is based on the portion of one that was built on the far wall of the original structure. These lean-to structures will protect the poles in the wall from the rain. We have completed an initial overview of the project, and I know it will be a success!

Felix Holmes with the movers from McKenzie House Movers of Lufkin. The barn was two of these roughly 14 square foot sections with a single roof. The other part of the barn, which has partially collapsed, is not visible in this picture. The long pieces of lumber are intended to hold the building together when it is transported. This is in northeastern Angelina County, roughly 30 miles from Chireno.

At Chireno, Felix talks to Mike McKenzie about the location of the barn. Sandra Fiske of the Chireno Historical Society is visible just beyond the pick-up. Sandra is one of those responsible for the maintenance of the property. The bell is from the Chireno Baptist Church building, which is to the left. The Halfway or Stagecoach Inn is located to the right. The Inn and Church building have also been moved to this property.

Author: Felix Holmes Jr.

CPSIA information can be obtained
at www.ICGtesting.com
Printed in the USA
LVHW050002070720
659826LV00017B/226